Mathematical Models: Population Genetics

Mathematical Models: Population Genetics

Dr. Ram Awadhesh Kumar

Lucky International
New Delhi - 110080

Mathematical Models: Population Genetics

ISBN- 978-93-83514-10-6

Rs - 595/

First Published -2017

Published by

Lucky International
H-16/1922, Sangam Vihar
New Delhi - 110080
Mob - 07838260289
E-mail-luckybk05@yahoo.co.in

Printed in
New Delhi

Contents

Chapter-1

INTRODUCTION

Historical Development of Genetics

Genetics is a very young branch barely three—quarters of a century old. In ancient times man had some vague idea of some general aspects of the problem of heredity. Genetics came into being with the Mendel's basic law of inheritance published in 1866. He used elementary probability theory to explain the transmission of qualitative traits in successive generations of garden peas.

Mathematical population genetics started with the Hardy Weinberg theorem in 1908. Since it describes the condition of equilibrium in a population, it is said to form the basis of "Population Statics". Later on three mathematical biologist' Fisher, Wright and Haldane emphasised on the study of population rather than the individual or family or group. They formulated the laws of change on gene frequencies and laid the foundation of "Population dynamics" in genetics.

In 1939 Etherington applied the theory of non-associative (linear) algebras in Mendelian genetics.

The history of mathematical biology reveals that population genetics is the dest branch of biology in which abstract algebraic models have been applied with success. Etherignton (4) introduced baric algebra, train, algebra, special train algebra and its commutative duplicate. Sehafer and Gowshor (8-10) introduced "Genetic algebras". The mathematical theory has been further developed by Goshor (8-10), Helgate (13-15), Reirsol, Heach (16-17) Worz-Buskeres (31) Abraham(1-2), Me Hale and Rigood (25).

The history of genetics will be incomplete if we do not include the development of molecular genetics which has recently come to the forefront. This branch also involved elementary mathematics in the beginning but later on for deeper insights required advanced mathematical analysis. The importance of the branch is that while physics enables a man to transform inorganic world directly, the molecular genetics (and its technical aspect genetic engineering) claims to transform the man and also the society. Uptill now man has developed genetics but in future genetics will develop the man. The impact of the branch on the society is so direct that its future development has raised many moral, ethical and legal questions.

Molecular genetics came into existence (in 1953) with the discovery of genetic material as a macromolecule DNA (dexoy riborucleic cuid) by Watson and Crick. DNA consists of two helically coiled polynucleotide chains bonded together crosswise by hydrogen bonding between a (adenine or guanine) and a pyrimidine (thymine or cytosine). Adenine, guanine, thymine, cytosine are nitrogeneous bases which are denoted by A, G, T C respectively. The restriction on the pairing of bases is imposed by the limitations of H-bonding of A to T and of G to C. For example, a sequence of bases in DNA may proceed as follows :

A – T
G – C
T – A
A – T
C – G
• •
• •
• •

We observe that each polypeptide chain can be obtained by making the interchanges A<–>C<–>G in the other. Hence each chain is called complementary to the other. The polynucleotide chains are enormously long. A typical chrommal DNA molecule in a human cell is composed of about five billion (5×10^9) pairs of nucleotides. DNA of any living being is determined by the sequences of four letters A, T, C, G. This is a kind of biological information contained in the genetic material of each cell.

DNA in any organism serves two fundamental purposes: duplication of a gene and the protein synthesis. In each process it preserves the biological information.

Genetics tells us that the density of a man is not determined by the astrological language written on a long piece of paper by a priest but it is written by the nature at the time of formation of zygote in the language whose words are sequences, each consisting of millions of the letters A, C, T. G. After that each book of life in the gene duplicates and in a grown up man we have million of copies of the book. By the help of information theory we can easily calculate the information contained in a single typical human gene. Roughly, this information can be written in alphabetical human language in four thousand volumes of books, each containing five hundred ordinary pages.

Algebraic models have also been applied to molecular genetics. Two important works in this field are those of Robert Rosen and Ronald Newbill.

2. Genetics

Definitions : Genetics is that branch of biological science which deals with the transmision of character from parents to offsprings.

The term Genetics was introduced by Bateson in 1906. It has been derived from the Greek word gene, which means to become or 'to grow into'. Therefore, genetics is the science of 'coming into being'.

2.1. Mendel's Laws

Mendel postulated following laws, now known as Mendel's lawof Heredity.

(*i*) Law of dominance : This law states, "when two homozygous individuals with one or more sets of contrasting characters are crossed the characters that appear in the F_1 hybrids are dominant characters and those that do not appear in F_1 are recessive characters.

(*ii*) Law of segregation (purity of gemetes) : This law states that when a pair of contrasting factors or genes or alleles are brought together in a heterozygote (hybrid) the two members of the allelic pair remain together without being contaminated and when gametes are formed from the hybrid, the two separate (out from each) and only one enters each gamete.

(*iii*) Law of independent assortment : If the inheritance of more than one pair of characters (two pairs or more) is-tudied simultaneously, the factors or genes for each pair of characters assort out independently. (of the other pairs.)

2.2. Population Genetics

Definition : Population genetics is that branch of genetics which deals with frequencies of alleles and genotypes in breeding groups of individuals.

Population genetics is based upon ideas which are essentially modifications of Mendel's ideas.

We define below the follow terms which are now accepted in the theory.

Gene : Gene is a particular hereditary determiner, located in a fixed location in the chromosome.

Chromosomes : Chromosomes are the carriers of gene which are arranged in a linear order in a single line All genes located in the same chromosome show linkage.

Autosomes : Chromosomes other than the sex chromosomes are known as autosomes.

Sex Chromosomes : Usually one pair of chromosomes carry, among others, genes determining the sex of the individual.

Homologous Chromosome : Pair of chromosomes in sexually reproducing organisms which carry alleles and are physically alike in shape, length, and position of centromere. Each member of a pair is called a homolog. Each parent contributes one of each pair homologous to their progeny.

Locus : A fixed position on a chromosomes occupied by given gene or one of its alleles is called a locus.

Alleles : A pair of genes located at corresponding positions on a pair of homologous chromosomes; these interest to determine a particular trait.

Genotype : The specific genetic constitution (gene mak up), expressed and latent, of a organism is called the genotype.

Phenotype : Phenotype is defined characteristic of an individual obeserved ir discernable by other means (i.e. tallness in garden peas, colour blindness or blood-type in man).

Gamete : A mature male or female reproductive cell (sperm or eggis called the gamete.

Gametogenesis : The formation ofthe gametes is called gemetogenesis.

Zygote : Azygote is the cell produced by the unionof two mature sex cell (gametes) in reproduction.

Homozygote : If a pair of alleles at a locus are identical (such as a_1, a_1), the individual is called the homozygote for that locus.

Hetrozygote : If a pair of a alleles at a locus are different(such as a_1, a_2), the individual is called the hetrozygote for that locus.

Genome : A complete set of chromosome (hence of genes), inherited as a unit from one parent is called a genome.

Monoploid of Haploid : An individual having only one genome is called monoloid or haploid.

Polyploid : An organism with more than two genomes is known as polyploid e.g. triploid, tetraploid, pentaploid, hexaploid etc.

Auto Polyploid : An autopolyploid is defined as a polyploid that has multiple and identical geneomes. A $2x$-ploid is an autopolyploid with set of identical genomes.

Linkage : The phenomenon of inheritance of a group of genes together is known as linkage. The linked genes retain their parental combination even in the offspring.

Recombination : The homologous chromosomes in a zygote while separatingin gamete production, break in identical places and exchange partners. This process is known as recombination.

Segregation : Segregation is defined as the separation of the paternal from maternal chromosomes a meiosis, and the consequent separation of alleles and their phenotypic differences as observed in the offspring.

Random Mating : If a population contains the genotypes $G_1, G_2.....G_1$ in proportions m_1, m_2......., m_1 amongst moles ($\Sigma m = 1$) and in proportions f_1, f_2,............., f_1 amongst the females ($\Sigma f = 1$); and the proportion of matings of the type G_1 (male)x Gj (female) is $m_1 f_1$, then mating is said to be random.

Gene Frequency : The relative proportions of alleles as represented in a breedingor random mating population are called gene frequencies.

Genetic Equilibrium : Genetic equilibrium is the condition in a group of interbreeding organism in which particular gene frequencies remain constant through succeeding generations.

Hardy-Weinberg Theorem : If the population produces the gametes (or genotypes) a_x in the proportion Px, then after (on) generation of the random mating the genetic (or genotypic array will be of the form

$$\{\Sigma_x P_x a_x\}^2 \quad ...(1)$$

and will remain the same in the subsequent generations.

Hardy-Weingberg Equilibrium : A population whose genotypic proportion is in accordance with Hardy-Weinberg theorem, is said to be in Hardy-Weinberg equilibrium.

Remark : A necessary and sufficient condition for Hardy-Weinberg equilibrium is that the frequency of each hetrozygote is given by twice geometric mean of the frequencies of the two corresponding homozygotes, as is immediately evident from (1).

2.3. Molecular Genetics

Recent advances in molecular genetics have revealed that the information inheritated by an organism is preserved and translated into proteins by three basic processes :

1. DNA : Duplication (or gene duplication).
2. DNA : m-RNA transcription.
3. Translation.

In what follows we describe these basic processes.

1. DNA : duplication (or gene duplication) : In duplication process the strands of DNA break up and each serves as a template for regaining its complementory strand. Thus after the first stage one gene gives rise towo identical genes. In the second stage each of the two genes gives rise to pair of genes i.e. four genes in all. Again in the next phase these four genes i.e. four genes in all. Again in the next phase these four genes gives rise to the eight ganes. Thus, the genes grow in a geometric progresion 2, 2^2, 2^3,............, 2^n, preserving the information (i.e. the sequence of nucleutidies). This leads to the growth of an organism preserving its hereditary properties.

2. DNA-m-RNA transcription **:** Under the presence of a suitable enzyme, a portion of single DNA chain acts as a template for the synthesis of a m-RNA sequences of A, U, C, G. The process is known as transcription. There is one-to-one correspondence between DNA Cistron (gene) and a transcribed m-RNA sequence. If when make the changes G □ C, G □ C, T □ A and A □ U in a DNA sequence we get the transcribed m-RN sequence. Alternatively we get the transcribed m-RNA sequence if we replace T by U in the complementary sequence of given DNA cistron.

3. Translation : Under the presence of a suitable enzyme, m-RNA synthesies a polypeptide chain. This process is called translation. Prolonged and hard work of many bio-chemists and biologists had led to the discovery of the simple rule of correpondence behind the process of translation. But this time the correpondence between the m-RNA and the translated polyeptide chain is many.

We know that m-RNA is a word up of 4 letters A, U, C, G and a polypeptide chain is also a word built up of 20 letters (20 aminoaid residues). Hence first we must seek a correspondence between the set X of four letters A,U, C, G and the set Y of 20 amino acids, which can be extended to the m-RNA sequence. First we note that the translation can not be defined by a relation from X to Y which is than a mapping. For then one of the letter of X will correspond to more one amino acid which implies that an m-RNA may synthesise many polyeptide chains. But this is not supported by in vitro or in vivo experience. Let us see a

Preface

Genetics is a very young branch barely three quarters of a century old. In ancient times man had some vague idea of some general aspects of the problem of heredity. Genetics came into being with the Mendel's basic law of inheritance published in 1866. He used elementary probability theory to explain the transmission of qualitative traits in successive generations of garden pea.

Mathematical population genetics started with the Hardy Weinberg theorem in 1908. Since it describes the condition of equilibrium in a population, it is said to form the basis of "Population Statistics". Later on three mathematical biologists Fisher, Wright and Haldane emphasized on the study of population rather than on the individual or family of group. They formulated the laws of change of gene frequencies and laid the foundation of "Population dynamics" in genetics.

There arc fivc chapters in this book. In the first chapter I have introduced some definitions, basis terms which are used in subsequent chapters.

In the second chapter, a matrix method of solving a nonlinear difference equation has been forwarded, about which well knew mathematical genesists J.B.S. Haldane had made a passing comment that a matrix method would not work here.

In the third chapter, it is shown that if there is an infinite random mating population of diploid individuals which differ at a single locus, the change in allele frequencies can be described through conic algebras. The possible form of a formula expressing the allele frequencies in the nth generation in the terms of those in the initial generation is obtained in the cases of two and three alleles with selection against a homozygous genotype.

In the fourth chapter equilibrium of a population of tetraploid individuals under a particular mode of selection are obtained using Brower's fixed point theorem. We have established that there is one and only one equilibrium state of a population under the mode of selection mentioned above. The result is on improvement upon the result of P.A. parson. Further we have formulated the problem of minimizing or maximizing the frequency of a gamete in the population and solved it for the particular mode of selection.

In the last chapter we have extended some of the results of fourth chapter to hexaploid population.

The present book is an embodiment of the researches carried on by me under the kind supervision of Dr. Mithilesh Kumar Singh, Professor, Department of Mathematics, Ranchi University, Ranchi. I am deeply indebted to him for his constant encouragement, guidance and immense patience during the period of research work.

I am grateful to Dr. R. C. Choudhary, Professor and Ex-Head Department of Mathematics, Ranchi University, Ranchi for inspiring me to initiate this book.

I must thank Prof. Ivar Heach (University of Bergen) for sending me the article [23] of P.A. parsons which enabled us to know the present status of book in algebra of tetraploidy under selection and some problems therein which we would solve and thus advance the book of chapter IV.

Due thanks are also due to late Dr. D. K. Singh, who sent reprints of several basic papers from Moscow in 1988. Finally, I thank all the members of the Department of Mathematics, Ranchi University, Ranchi for their cordial assistance.

Dr. Ram Awadhesh Kumar
Principal, R. C. S. College, Manjhaul,
L. N. M. U. Darbhanga,
Bihar

well-defined mapping on the set X^2 or X^3 to the set Y, where,

X^2 = The set of all two letters words xy such that x or y has four Values A, U, C, G.

X^3 = The set of all three letter words xyz where each of x, y, z has four Values A,U, C, G.

Clearly X^2 has 16 (< 20) elements and

X^3 has $4 \times 4 \times 4 = 64$ (> 20) elements.

Thus, we may expect a mapping on X^3 to Y.

The three words such as A U U, U C G, are called codons.

The next question now is the correspondence(popularly known as codon assignment) which can be established and realised. Khorana used many regular copolymers in cell-free protein synthesizing systems to determine code assignments. He took the m-RNA sequence $(U-C)_n$ = UCU – CUC –UCU and obtained the polypeptide chain.

Ser – Leu — Ser— Leu

This indicated that UCU codes for ser and CUC codes for Leu-with the help of these many in vitro and in vivo methods they have obtained all the codon assignements except the three UAA, UAG, UGA which are called chain terminating codons, for their inclusion in any m-RN results in the abrupt termination of the message at the point of their location. The genetic code is degenerate in the sense that more than one codon corresponds to the same amino acid. This fact can be mathematically expressed by saying that the mapping on the set x^3 of codons to the set y of amino acids is many one. Also the code is universal.

The most important correspondence of codon assignment law is that we can identify the polypetide chain produced by an m-RNA by means of a colinearity between m-RN base sequence and the amino acid sequence. Thus it leads (leads) one gene (one DNA cistron) one polypeptide chain hypothesis (which is a modification of one gene-one protein hypothesis). Mathematically if X-denotes the set of all single stranded DNA cistrons free of TAA, TAG, TGA (or o all m-RNA's frcc of UAA, UAG, UGA) and Y denote the set of all polyeptide chains, a many one mapping of exists which maps X onto Y. The biosynthesis of protein from DNA can be shown by the following diagram :

A DNA Cistron (gene) □ an m-RNA sequence □ a polypeticle chain. More than one DNA cistrons □ many polypeptide chains □ a protein molecule.

It is remarkable that informations contained in the genes are also preserved in the protein (Produced by the genes) in form of amino acid sequence with a loss to a certain degree which can be determined by the degeneracy of the genetic code.

In the light of molecular genetics we have following modified definitions :

Chromosome : A chromosome is a chain macromolecule consisting of four nucleotides-edenine (A), guanine (0), Cystosine (C) and thymine (T), where each nucleotide may be repeated. Thus a chromosome may be treated as a cypher constructed from an alphabet of four letters.

Gene : A portion of chromosome (a sequence of nucleotides) which can code polypeptide chain (sequence of amino acids) is calleda gene. More accurately a gene is a set of nucleotides sequence which can code the same polypeptide chain.

3. Algebraic Preliminaries

3.1. Notations : We shall use following notations :

N — The set of natural numbers

K — An arbitrary field.

L — An extension of the field K

R — Field of real numbers

C — Field of complex numbers

V — Vector space

< U > — Subspace spanned by a subset U of a vector space V

K — $\{x_1, x_2, \ldots\ldots\ldots x_n\}$ algebra of all polynomiales in a associative non-comulative indeterminates over the field K.

GH — Subspace spanned by all gh, g ∉ G, h ∉ H, G, H being any two subset of vector space V.

3.2. Definitions and Important Results from Algebra

Definitions

Non Associative Alorebra : Let A be a vector space over a field K. A is non-associative algebra if a mutiplication xy is defined in A, $\forall\ x, y$ □ A, subject to the following conditions :

1. Distributivity

   $x\,(y + z) = xy + xz$

   $(y + z) = yx + zx, \ \forall\ x, y = z$ □ A

2. Compatibility with scalar multiplications

   i.e. ʟ $(xy) = ($ʟ$x)y = x\,($ʟ$y)$

$\forall$ x, y □ A, $\forall$ ʟ □ K.

Remark : (*i*) A has the structure of both a vector space and a non-associative ring.

(*ii*) A is not necessarily associative.

Associative Algebra : A non-associative algebra A is called associative if

$$(xy)z = x\,(yz), \forall \text{ □□}, y, z \text{ □ A}.$$

Finite Dimensional Non-Associative Algebra Over a Field K :

(*i*) A non-associative algebra A is called finite dimensional if the underlying vector space of A is finite dimensional or equivalently.

(*ii*) Let A be a finite dimensional vector space over a field K with basis elements $e_1, e_2, \ldots\ldots\ldots\ldots\ldots\ldots e_n$.

A is called an algebra if a multiplication in A is defined by the multiplication of basis elements.

$$e_i e_j = \sum_{k=1}^{n} e_{ijk} = \in e_k \text{ , where i, j} = 1, 2, \ldots\ldots, n \text{ and } e_{ijk} \text{ □ 2K.}$$

and its bilinear extension to A.

Non Commutative Algebra : The algebra which is not necessarily commutative is called non commutative algebra.

Since the algebras occuring is genetics are usually finite dimensional and not associative, the term algebra without qualification will denote a non-associative finite dimensional non-commutative algebra throughout the thesis.

Subalgebras Ideals and Homomorphism : The concepts in the theory of associative algebra, which are independent of associativity have unambiguous analouges in the theory of non-associative algebras.

If for G, HCA, GH denotes the subspace of A spanned by all gh, g □G, h □H, we have the following definitions :

Subalgebra of A : A subspace U of A is called a subalgebra if UUU.

Ideals in an Algebra :

Left Side : A subspace I of A is called a left ideal if A □ I.

Right Deal : A subspace I of A is called a right ideal if IA □ I.

Ideal : A subspace I of A is called an ideal if AI □ I and IA □ I.

Algebra, Homomorphism : Let A and B algebras over the field K and

f.

A □ B be a mapping. F is called an algebra homomorphism if the following conditions are satisfied $\forall\, x, y$ A, $k \Box$ K.

(*i*) f preserve additions

i.e. $f(x+y) = f(x) + f(y)$.

(*ii*) f preserves multiplications by scalars

i.e. $f(kx) = kf(x)$

and (3) f preserves bilinear multiplications

i.e. $f(xy) = f(x) f(y)$

Kernal of a Homomorphism : Let A and B be two algebras over K. Then the Kernel of a homomorphism f: A $\Box$ B is defined as :

$$\text{Ker } f = \{x \Box \text{ A } : f(x) = 0\}\text{s}$$

Ker f is an ideal of A.

Quotient Algebra **:** Let I be an ideal of an algebra A. The quotient algebra A/f is the set of all vector space cosets.

$a + 1, a \Box$ A in which the algebraic operations are defined as follows:

$$\forall \text{ K} \Box \text{ K}, a, s \Box \text{ A}$$

$$(a+1) + (b+\text{I}) = (a+b) + \text{I}$$

$$\text{K}(a+\text{I}) = \text{K}(a+\text{I})$$

and $$(a+\text{I})(b+\text{I}) = ab + \text{I}.$$

Direct sum (or Direct Product) of Algebra : Let $A_1, A_2, \ldots\ldots.. A_r$ be algebras over the field K. Let $A = A_1 \Box A_2 \Box \ldots\ldots \Box Ar$ [Or $A = A_1 \Box A_2 \Box \ldots.$ $\Box A_r$ be the vector space direct sum (or product).

A becomes an algebra if we define the multiplication in A as follows:

$(a_1, a_2, \ldots\ldots\ldots\ldots, a_r)(b_1, b_2, \ldots\ldots\ldots, b_r)$

$= (a_1, b_1, a_2 b_2, \ldots\ldots\ldots\ldots\ldots\ldots a_r b_r)$, where $a_1, b_1 \Box A_1$

$i = 1, 2, \ldots\ldots. r$ and

the juxtaposition denotes a mutlplication in the component algebra A_1. A equipped with this law of multiplication is called the direct sum (or product) of the algebras $A_1, A_2, \ldots\ldots, A_r$.

Tensor Product of Algebra : Let $A_1, A_2, \ldots\ldots\ldots\ldots, A_r$ be algebras over K with dimensions $n_1, n_2, \ldots\ldots. n_r$ and $A_1 \Box A_2 \Box \ldots\ldots\ldots. \Box A_r$ be the tensor product of vector spaces underyling $A_1, A_2, \ldots\ldots\ldots A_r$. Each element of the tensor product can be represented as :

$$\sum_{i=1} x_{\text{H}} \Box \ldots\ldots\ldots. \Box x_{ri}$$

with linearly indepedent elements

$$x_{\alpha_1} \in \text{Ai}, \forall \varkappa = 1, 2, \ldots.. r$$

The tensor product $A_1 + A_2 + \ldots\ldots + A_r$ with the multiplication defined by :

$$(\sum_{j\in j} y_j\, x.........xy_{rj})$$

****

is an algebra and this algebra is called the tensor product of the lgebras $A_1, A_2, ..., A_r$.

Left and Right Transformations is an Algebra : Let A be an n-dimensional algebra over a field K. Also, let M be the the algebra of linear mapping of A into itself. The linear mappings $\varkappa_x$: A □ A, defined by $\varkappa_x(a) = xa$, a □A and R_x : A □ A defined by $R_x(a) = ax$, a □A are called the left and right transformations of A induced by x □ A.

Transformation Algebra of an Algebra A : Let F (A) be the subalgebra of M which is generated by all $\varkappa_x$, R_x, x □A and the identity of A. The subalgebra F (A) of M is called the transformation alegebra of A.

Remarks : (*i*) A is commutative if $\varkappa_x = R_x$

(*ii*) A is associative if the linear mappings of A into M defined by by ₣ : x □ $\varkappa_x$ and : ¥ : x □ R_x, x □ A, are algebra Homomorphism.

Subalgebra of a Transformation Algebra : Let B be any subalgebras of A. Then B is the subalgebra of F (A) generated by all left and right transformation $\varkappa_n$ and R_b, b □ B.

Remark : B* may be proper subalgebra of F (A) if A does not contain a unit element.

Powers in an Algebra : We shall use the following definitions which appear in (31).

Let A be an algebra over a field K.

Let x □ A, then

(*i*) $i_k = x$, $x^{+1} x = (x^r)$, r □N are called the left principal powers of x and

(*ii*) $x^1 = s$

$x^{x+1} = (x^x)x, r \in$ N are called the right principal powers of x.

Principal Powers of a Subalgebra of A : Let U □ A be a subalgebra of A, then

(*i*) $1_U = U$,

$^{r+1}U = < U\,(^rU) > r$ □ N, are called the left principal powers of U,

(*ii*) $U^1 = U$,

$U^{r+1} = < (U^r)\, U > r$ □N.

are called the right principal powers of U.

(*iii*) $U(1) = U$,

$U(R+1) = < UU(R), U(r) U >, r EN$

are called principal powers of U

Plenary Powers of an Element of A : The plenary powers of an element x □ A are defined as

$$x^{[1]} = x$$

$$x^{[x+1]} = x^{[r]} x^{[r]}, r \square N.$$

Plenary powers of a subalgebra U of A : The plenary powers of a subalgebra U of A are defined as :

$$U^{[1]} = U,$$

$$U^{(r+1)} = < U^{[r]} U^{[r]} > r \notin N.$$

Idempotents in an Algebra (or in a Semi-Group) : An element of an algebra (or a semi group) is called an idempotent if $e^2 = e$.

Nilpotent Elements : An element x of an algebra A is called.

(*i*) Left nil potent of index K if $k_x = 0$ but $k^{-1}x$ □ 0 and

(*ii*) Right nil potent of index k iff $x^k = 0$ but x^{k-1} □ 0.

Nil Potent Subalgebras : A subalgebra U of a is called

(*i*) Left nil potent of index k if $k_U = < 0 >$ but ^{k-1}u □ $< 0 >$

(*ii*) Right nil potent of index k if $U^k = < 0 >$ but U^{k-1} □ $< 0 >$ and

(*iii*) Nil potent of index K if $U^{(k)} = < 0 >$ but $U^{(k-1)} < 0 >$

Remark : In commutative case left and right ideals, subalgebras and nil potent elements coincide.

Nilideal : If every element of an ideal is Nilpotent, the ideal is called nil.

Solva Ble Subalgebra : A subalgebra U of a is called solvable of index k if :

$$U^{[k]} = < 0 > \text{ but } U^{[k-1]} \square < 0 >$$

4. ***Algebra Applied in Population Genteics :*** In this section we record different types of algebras related to inneritance without solution.

Definitions :

4.1. Domestic Algebra and Segeration Confficients

Let us a consider an infinite random mating population of diploid or 2r - ploid organisms which differ at one or several loci. In general, let $a_1, a_2, \ldots\ldots\ldots, a_n$ be genetically distinct gametes with frequiencies p_1, $p_2, \ldots\ldots\ldots\ldots, p_n$ respectively. Then the state of the population is represented by :

$$\sum_{i=1}^{n} p_1 a_1 \text{, where } \sum_{i=1}^{n} p_1 = 1 \qquad ...(8)$$

Let a_i, a_j mate randomly to form the zygote $a_i a_j$ for $i, j = 1, 2, ... n$. On gametogenesis, let $a_i a_j$ give rise to gametes $a_1, d_2, ..., a_n$ with probebilities λi_{jk}. We express this fact by writing :

$$a_i a_j = \sum_{k=1}^{n} {}^{\lambda} ijk \ a_k \ \text{ for } i, j = 1, 2, ...n..... \qquad (9)$$

λ_{ijk} are called segregation coeficients (or rates).

If the loci under consideration are autosomal (*i.e.* related to autosomal chromosomes) then

$$a_i a_j = a_j a_i$$

i.e. $\lambda_{ijk} = \lambda_{jik}$

Such λ_{jik} are called symmetric.

If the loci are sex-linked (i.e. related to sex chromosomes). Then in general

$$\lambda_{ijk} \square \lambda_{jik}$$

In such a situation λ_{ijk} are called osymetric.

Mendelian Segregation Coefficates (Rates) : According to Mendel's laws the mode of segregation of genotypos a_i, a_j is :

$$a_i a_j = \frac{1}{2}(a_i + a_j) \qquad ....(10)$$

i.e. $\lambda_{ijk} = \dfrac{1}{2}$ if $k = i$ or j

$= 0$ if $k_\lambda = i, j$

such segregation coefficents i_{jk} are called simple mendelian.

We take the symbols $a_1, a_2.....a_n$ as basis elements of a vector space V over B. If a multiplication in V is defined by (10) and its bilinear extension to $v \times v$, v becomes an algebra G called a gametic algebra. Clearly the gametic algebra is commutative or non commutative according as the segregation sufficient λ_{ijk} are the symatric or not necessarly symetric.

The notion of gametic algebra leads to the following generalisation.

4.2. Stochastic and Baric Algebras

Let A be an algebra over k = B or C, then A is called a stochastic algebra iff it admits a basis $a_1, a_2, ...a_n$ such that the multiplication constants λ_{ijk} defined by

$$a_i a_j = \sum_{k=1}^{n} {}^{\lambda} ijk\, a_k$$

satisfy the following conditions :

(*i*) 0 £ $Ł_{ijk}$ £ 1 ...(*ii*)

(*ii*) $\sum_{k=1}^{n} {}^{\lambda}{}_{ijk} = 1, i, j = 1, 2, \ldots\ldots n.$

Clearly a stchastic algebra A over K admits a non-trivial algebra homomorphism *w* given by

$$w\,(a_i) = 1, \text{ for } i = 1,2, \ldots\ldots\ldots, n.$$

Hence we are led to

Peric algebra : An algebra a over a field *k* is called baric if it admits a aestrivial algebra homomorphism,

$$w : \text{A} □ \text{K}.$$

w is called the weight homomorphism

4.3 Commutative Baric Algebras

Let 'A' be a accumutative baric algebra. The class of baric algebras is much wider than that of algebras describing conerete genetic situations. An algebra belonging to the later class admits a canonical basic with respect to which the matrices representing left transformations corresponding to basis with respect to which the matricas representing left transformations corresondingto basis elements are all triangular. Such an algebra is called a conshor genetic algebra which we define below :

Gonshor Genetic Algebra : Let A be an (n + 1) dimensional algebra over *k*.A is called Gonshor Genetic if the extended algebra A_L (L being a suitable extension of *k*) admits a basic c_2, c_1, c_1,......c_n such that the multiplication constants $Ł_{ijk}$ given by

$$e_i e_j = \sum_{k=0}^{n} \lambda_{ijk} c_k\ ,$$

$i, j = 0, 1, 2, \ldots\ldots. n$, have the following properties :

(*i*) $Ł_{eee}$ = I,

(*ii*) $Ł_{ojk}$ =0, for $k < j$ and

(*iii*) $Ł_{ijk}$ = 0, for *k* £ max (*i*, *j*) ...(12)

if $i, j > 0$

Note : (*i*) The basis ($c_0, c_1, c_2, \ldots\ldots c_n$) given by (12) is called a canonical basis.

(*ii*) A Gonshor genetic algebra is baric with weight homomorphism w given by

$w(c_0) = 1, w(c_1) = c, i = 1, 2, \ldots\ldots n.$

Schafer GeneticAlgebra : Let A be a finite dimensional baric algebra with weight homomorphism w. Let F (A) be the transformation algebra of A.Then A is called schafer genetic if for every transformation $T \in$ F (A) with representation

$T = f \rtimes \times 1, R \times 2, R \times 5$ the coefficients of the characteristic polynomial of T are functions of $w(x_1), w(x_2) \ldots\ldots, w(x_2)$ only.

4.3. Gametic Algebra : Inheritance with Selection

Let $a_1, a_2, \ldots\ldots\ldots\ldots a_n$ be n gametes. Let the segregation behaviour of the zygote $a_i\, a_j$ be

$$a_i a_j = \sum_{k=1}^{n} \lambda_{ijk}\, ak \;;\; \sum \lambda_{ijk} = 1$$

in absance of selection.

If only a fraction w_{ij} of the zygotes $a_i a_j$ is survived, we express this fact by formal expression.

$$a_i a_j = w_{ij} \sum_{k=1}^{n} \lambda_{ijk}\, a_k \qquad \ldots(i)$$

are called viabilities.

We take $a_1, a_2 \ldots\ldots a_n$ as basis elements of a real vector grace A with law of multiplication(1), then A becomes a non-associative algebra.

An element

$x = x_1 a_1 + x_2 a_2 + \ldots\ldots\ldots\ldots + x_n a_n$ of A represents the state of a population on, if x_1 is are non-negative not all zero such that they represent the proportions of the garetes a_1's.

x^2 represents the state of the filial population.

Define the norm of x by

$$\|x\| = |x_1| + |x_2| + \ldots\ldots + |x_n|$$

If $\|x\| = 1$, x will be called unit vector.

If x is a Unit vector x_1 denote the frequenc of the Gametic a_1.

Two vectors x and y are said to be equivalent (x ∀ y) if $x = ry$, for some real positive r.

The evoluation equation is given by

$$x^{(1)} = x^2$$

$$x^{(r)} = x^{(x-1)}\, x^{(x-1)},\ r = 2, 3, \ldots\ldots$$

Note : The usual evoluation equation is :

$$x^{(1)} = \frac{x^2}{\| x^2 \|} \qquad \ldots(2)$$

where $\quad \bar{x} = \dfrac{x}{\| x \|}.$

But it is easy to see that

$$\bar{x}^n = \frac{x^{(n)}}{\| x^{(n)} \|}$$

Hence due to simplicity we consider (2) instead of (2).

Theorem-1 : Gametic algebra of polypoidy under selection is non-associatve Banach algebra with respect to the norm defined by

$$\left\| \sum_{i=1}^{n} x_i a_i \right\| = \sum_{i=1}^{n} | x_i |$$

Proof : It is sufficient to show that ∆∆ ∆∆ is sub-multiplicative we have

$$\Delta\Delta y \Delta\Delta \left\| \sum_j x_i\, a_i \sum_j y_j\, a_j \right\|$$

$$= \left\| \sum_{i+j} x_i\, y_j \sum_k \lambda_{ijk}\, a_k \right\|$$

Where $\quad w_{ij} = p_{ijk}^{k} = \text{L}_{ijk},\ a_i a_j = \sum_{k=1} p_{ijk}\, a_k \ \ (0 < w_{ij} < 1, \sum_{k=1}^{n} p_{ink} = 1)$

$$i.e. \|xy\| \le \sum_k \sum_{ij} |x_i||y_i| \sum_k \lambda\text{KJK} < \sum{}_J 1 \times {}_1 1 \sum_J |x_i| = \|x\| \|y\|$$

4.4. Notivation for the Present Work

Several situations in population genetics without selection have been described through genetic algebras. Genetic algebras (e.g. Gomeshorand Sebafer algebras) are non-associative and Attracted several worker viz. Sehafor, Goeshor,Holgate, Abraham; Worz-Buskros, Singh. Unfortunately when selection is allowed the genetic algebra lose many nice properties viz. Sehafereity, Triasgularity, livearizability etc. In presence of selection, only the comic property of the algebra is retained Vide [25]. In this case the inheritance can be better described by the techniques of functional analysis then by the algebras. In the present thesis our aim is to describe inheritance is presence of selection and so we have to depend largely on analysis. For this, motivation mainly came from the work of Singh and Prasad [30] and worz-Baskeres [31]. The motivation to studyMendelian inheritance in presence of selection came from Haldane [11] Edwards [5], and Ringwood [25].

Chapter-2

LINEARIZATION OF THE DIFFERENCES EQUATIONS FOR SIMPLE INBREADING SYSTEMS

1. Introduction

The state of a random mating genetic populationis characterized by the frequencies of genotypes. The dynamics of the population is described by the change of these frequencies from generation to generation. The change of frequency from a generation to the filial generation is usually represented by a quadratic difference equation. A wide variety of concerete situations with random mating and absence of differential selection is described by quadratic transformations in genetic algebra. For a complete survey we refer to [31]. For the most general situation in genetics of polyploidy we refe to [27]. Further it has been described in[13]. [1]. [2] and [28] that a quadratic transformation in a genetic algebra can be linearised. Unfortunately the frequency changes of genotypes of genetic population mating randomly with selection can not be described by genetic algebras. In fact no general formula or method is known for obtaining the frequencies of genotypes of a the generation in terms of those of initial generation. The basic reason behind this is that the form of transformation describing the frequency changes is not quadratic but it is rational. In this thesis we apply matrix method to obtain the genotype frequencies in in the generation in terms of those of filial generation of a genetic population (with selection) described by Haldone [H].

1.2. The difference Equations

In [11] Haldone describes the inheritance of inbreeding population by the equations [System (4) in his paper]

$$x_{n+1} = \frac{(1-k)x_n + \frac{1}{4}y_n}{1-kx_n - lk_n} \qquad ...(a)$$

$$y_{n+1} = \frac{\frac{1}{2}y_n}{1-kx_n - lz_n} \qquad ...(b)...(1)$$

$$z_{n+1} = \frac{(1-l)_{zn} + \frac{1}{4}y_n}{1-kx_n - lz_n} \qquad ...(c)$$

where k and l are measure of selection such that $0 < k, i < 1$.

x_n, y_n, z_n and $x_{n+1}, y_{n+1}, z_{n+1}$ are the frequencies of genotypes in the nth and $(n+1)$th generation respectively.

Such that $x_n + y_n + z_n = 1 = x_{n+1} + y_{n+1} + z_{n+1}$

Also extending a hypothesis of Hayman and Mather [12] about selfing he obtain the difference equations :

$$U_n x_{n+1} = (1 - K)(x_n + \frac{1}{4} y_n)$$

$$U_n y_{n+1} = \frac{1}{2} y_n \qquad \text{...(2)}$$

$$U_n e_{n+1} = (1 - 1)(z_n + \frac{1}{2} y_n)$$

$$u_n = 1 - k(x_n + \frac{1}{2} y_n) - 1(z_n + \frac{1}{2} y_n)$$

when $\quad k = 1 = 1 - x.$

Equation (2) reduces to Hayman and Mather equations corrected by Haldane. He remarks that the modified equation is non-linear and can not be solved by Matrix method (Page 62, in [3]),

Clearly this remark also applies to the equations (1) and (2). In this chapter we show that both (1) and (2) can be solved by matrix method.

2.1. Solution System (2)

Dividing (a) by (b) and (c) by (b)

$$\frac{x_{n+1}}{y_{n+1}} = 2(1-k)\frac{x_n}{y_n} + \frac{1}{2}$$

and $$\frac{z_{n+1}}{y_{n+1}} = 2(1-l)\frac{z_n}{y_n} + \frac{1}{2}$$

If $$\frac{x_n}{y_n} = u_n, \frac{x_n}{y_n} = v_n$$

and $\dfrac{x_{n+1}}{y_{n+1}} = u_{n+1} ; \dfrac{z_{n+1}}{y_{n+1}} = v_{n+1}$ the above equations can be put into the matrix from as :

$$=\begin{bmatrix} U_{n+1} \\ 1 \end{bmatrix} = \begin{bmatrix} 2(1-k) & \frac{1}{2} \\ 0 & 1 \end{bmatrix} \begin{bmatrix} u_n \\ 1 \end{bmatrix}$$

$$\begin{bmatrix} V_{n+1} \\ 1 \end{bmatrix} = \begin{bmatrix} 2(1-l) & \frac{1}{2} \\ 0 & 1 \end{bmatrix} \begin{bmatrix} V_n \\ 1 \end{bmatrix}$$

Put, $n = 0, 1, 2, 3, \ldots\ldots.n.$

$$\begin{bmatrix} u_1 \\ 1 \end{bmatrix} = A \begin{bmatrix} u_0 \\ 1 \end{bmatrix} \text{ where } A = \begin{bmatrix} 2(1-k) & \frac{1}{2} \\ 0 & 1 \end{bmatrix}$$

$$\begin{bmatrix} U_2 \\ 1 \end{bmatrix} = A \begin{bmatrix} U_1 \\ 1 \end{bmatrix} = A.A \begin{bmatrix} U_0 \\ 1 \end{bmatrix} = A^2 \begin{bmatrix} u_0 \\ 1 \end{bmatrix}$$

$$\begin{bmatrix} U_3 \\ 1 \end{bmatrix} = A \begin{bmatrix} u_2 \\ 1 \end{bmatrix} = A.A^2 \begin{bmatrix} u_0 \\ 1 \end{bmatrix} = A^3 \begin{bmatrix} u_0 \\ 1 \end{bmatrix}$$

$$\begin{bmatrix} U_n \\ 1 \end{bmatrix} = A^n \begin{bmatrix} u_0 \\ 1 \end{bmatrix}$$

$$\begin{bmatrix} u_n \\ 1 \end{bmatrix} = \begin{bmatrix} 2(1-k) & \frac{1}{2} \\ 0 & 1 \end{bmatrix}^n \begin{bmatrix} u_0 \\ 1 \end{bmatrix}$$

Similarly $$\begin{bmatrix} V_n \\ 1 \end{bmatrix} = \begin{bmatrix} 2(1-l) & \frac{1}{2} \\ 0 & 1 \end{bmatrix}^n \begin{bmatrix} v_0 \\ 1 \end{bmatrix}$$

We know that

$$\begin{bmatrix} a_1 & a_2 \\ 0 & 1 \end{bmatrix}^n = \begin{bmatrix} a_1^n & \frac{a_1^n - 1}{a_1 - 1} \times a_2 \\ 0 & 1 \end{bmatrix}$$

\

$$\begin{bmatrix} U_n \\ 1 \end{bmatrix} = \begin{bmatrix} (2-2k)^n & \dfrac{(2-2k)^n}{2(1-2k)} \\ 0 & 1 \end{bmatrix} \begin{bmatrix} U_o \\ 1 \end{bmatrix}$$

$$\begin{bmatrix} u_n \\ 1 \end{bmatrix} = \begin{bmatrix} (2-2k)^n u_0 & + \dfrac{(2-2k)^n - 1}{2(1-2k)} \\ 0 & \end{bmatrix}$$

i.e. $$u_n = (2-2k)^n u_0 + \frac{(2-2k)^n - 1}{2(1-2k)} \qquad ...(3)$$

Similarly $$v_n = (2-2l)^n y^n v_0 + \frac{(2-2l)^n - 1}{2(1-2l)} \qquad ...(4)$$

Clearly $$y_n = \frac{1}{1+u_n+v_n} \qquad ..(5)$$

putting the value of u_n and v_n from (3) and (4) in (5) we get

$$y_n = \cfrac{1}{\dfrac{2(1-2k)(2-2k)^n_{u_0} + (2-2k)^2 - 1}{2(1-2k)} + \dfrac{2(1-2l)(2-2l)^n_{v_0} + (2-2l)^n + (2-2l)^n - 1}{2(1-2l)} + 1}$$

$$y_n = \frac{2(1-2k)(1-2l)}{2(1-21)(1-2k)(2-2k)^n_{u_0}[(1-2l)\{(2-2k)^n - 1\}] + 2(1-2k)(1-21)(2-21)^n v_0 + [(1-2k)\{(2-21)^n - 1\}] + 2(1-2k)(1-21)}$$

$$y_n = \frac{2(1-2k)(1-2l)\,y_0}{2(1-2l)(1-2k)(2-2k)^n x_0 + [(1-2l)\{(2-2k)^n - 1\}]y_0 + 2(1-2k)(1-21)(1-21)(2-21)^n c_0 + [(1-2k)\{(2-21\}^n - y_0] + 2(1-2k)(1-21)y_0}$$

2.2. Solution : System (3)

We have $$\frac{x_{n+1}}{y_{n+1}} = (1-k)(2\frac{x_n}{y_n}+\frac{1}{2})$$

$$\frac{z_{n+1}}{y_{n+1}} = (1-l)(Za\frac{z_n}{y_n}+\frac{1}{2})$$

If $= \frac{x_n}{y_n} = a_n, \frac{z_n}{y_n} = b_n$; then the above equations can be put into the matrix form :

$$\begin{bmatrix} a_{n+1} \\ 1 \end{bmatrix} = \begin{bmatrix} 2(1-k) & \frac{1}{2}(1-k) \\ 0 & 1 \end{bmatrix} \begin{bmatrix} a_n \\ 1 \end{bmatrix}$$

$$\begin{bmatrix} b_{n+1} \\ 1 \end{bmatrix} = \begin{bmatrix} 2(1-l) & \frac{1}{2}(1-l) \\ 0 & 1 \end{bmatrix} \begin{bmatrix} b_n \\ 1 \end{bmatrix}$$

put, $n = 0, 1, 2, 3, \ldots\ldots\ldots n$.

$$\begin{bmatrix} a_1 \\ 1 \end{bmatrix} = B\begin{bmatrix} a_0 \\ 1 \end{bmatrix}; \text{ where } B = \begin{bmatrix} 2(1-k) & \frac{1}{2}(1-k) \\ 0 & 1 \end{bmatrix}$$

$$\begin{bmatrix} a_2 \\ 1 \end{bmatrix} = B\begin{bmatrix} a_1 \\ 1 \end{bmatrix} = B.B\begin{bmatrix} a_0 \\ 1 \end{bmatrix} = B^2\begin{bmatrix} a_0 \\ 1 \end{bmatrix}$$

$$\begin{bmatrix} a_3 \\ 1 \end{bmatrix} = B\begin{bmatrix} a_2 \\ 1 \end{bmatrix} = B.B^2\begin{bmatrix} a_0 \\ 1 \end{bmatrix} = B^3\begin{bmatrix} a_0 \\ 1 \end{bmatrix}$$

$$\begin{bmatrix} a_n \\ 1 \end{bmatrix} = B^n\begin{bmatrix} a_0 \\ 1 \end{bmatrix}$$

$$\begin{bmatrix} a_n \\ 1 \end{bmatrix} = \begin{bmatrix} 2(1-k) & \frac{1}{2}(1-k) \\ 0 & 1 \end{bmatrix}^n \begin{bmatrix} a_0 \\ 1 \end{bmatrix}$$

Similarly

$$\begin{bmatrix} b_n \\ 1 \end{bmatrix} = \begin{bmatrix} 2(1-l) & \frac{1}{2}(1-l) \\ 0 & 1 \end{bmatrix}^n \begin{bmatrix} b_n \\ 1 \end{bmatrix}$$

We know that

$$\begin{bmatrix} a_1 & a_2 \\ 0 & 1 \end{bmatrix}^n = \begin{bmatrix} a_1^n & \frac{a_1^n - 1}{a_1 - 1} a_2 \\ 0 & 1 \end{bmatrix}$$

\ $$\begin{bmatrix} a_n \\ 1 \end{bmatrix} = \begin{bmatrix} 2^n(1-k)^n & \frac{2^n(1-k)^n - 1}{2(1-k)-1} + \frac{1}{2}(1-k) \\ 0 & 1 \end{bmatrix} \begin{bmatrix} a_0 \\ 1 \end{bmatrix}$$

$$\begin{bmatrix} a_n \\ 1 \end{bmatrix} = \begin{bmatrix} 2^n(1-k)^n a_0 + \frac{2^n(1-k)^n - 1}{2(1-k)-1} \cdot \frac{1}{2}(1-k) \\ 1 \end{bmatrix}$$

\ $$a_n = 2^n(1-k)^n u_o + \frac{2^n(1-k)^n - 1}{2(1-k)-1} + \frac{1}{2}(1-k) \qquad ...(7)$$

Similarly,

$$b_n = 2^n(1-l)^n b_0 + \frac{2^n(1-l)^n - 1}{2(1-l)-1} + \frac{1}{2}(1-l) \qquad ...(8)$$

We have $$y_n = \frac{1}{1 + a_n + b_n} \qquad ...(9)$$

Putting the value of a_n and b_n from (7) and (8) in (9) we get, after simplification.

$$y_n = \frac{1}{1 + 2^n(1-k)^n u_0 + \frac{2^n(1-k)^n - 1}{2(1-k)-1} + \frac{1}{2}(1-k) + 2^n(1-l)^n b_0 + \frac{2^n(1-l)^n - 1}{2(1-l)-1} + \frac{1}{2}(1-l)}$$

$y_n = [2\,(2k-l)\,(2l-1)y_0]\,[2\,(2k-1)\,(2l-1)\,y_0 + 2^n.\,2\,(1-k)^n$
$(2k-1)\,(2l-1)x_0 + \{2^n\,(1-k)^n - 1\}\,(2l-1)\,(1-k)\,y_0$
$+\,2.2^n\,(1-l)^n\,(2k-1)\,(2l-1)z_0 + \{2^n\,(1-l)^n - 1\}(2k-1)\,(1-l)y_0]^{-1}$
$y_n = [2\,(2k-1)(2l-1)y_0][4k-1-k-1)y_0 + (2-2k)^n\,(2l-1)$
$\{2\,(2k-1)k_0 - (1-k)\,y_0\} + (2-2l)^n\,(2k-1)\,\{2\,(2l-1)\,z_0 - (1-l)y_0\}]^{-1}$

The values of y_n obtained in (6) and (10) are in agreement with those of Haldane [11] in equation (10) and (15). The factor (2K – 1) is missing in Haldane's $(2k-1)$ equation (10).

Remark : The contents of this chapter have been published in 'The Mathematics Student' [21].

Chapter-3

DIFFERENCE EQUATION DESCRIBING THE INHERITANCE OF DIPLOIDS

1. Introduction

The formula expressing the gene frequencies in the nth generation of large random mating population in terms of those in the initial generation has been obtained for alarge numberof situations without selection in population genetics through non-associative algebras. For a complete survey we refer to Worz Busekro [31]. For further development we refer to Holgate and Machado [15] and Singh [27].

In this chapter we show that a closed form formula expressing the gene frequencies in the nth generation of a genetic population in terms of those in the initial generation in presence of selection difficult to obtain even in simple cases. However we have obtained a possible form of such a formula.

2. Description of Inheritance Through Non-associative Algebras

Let us consider a linear space A over the real field R with a basis a_1, a_2, a_3,......a_n. An element $x_1a_1 + x_2a_2 +$...........$x_n a_n$, x_1 being positive real numbers of a A will represent the state of the genetic population, if a_1,a_2............., a_n represent genetically distinct gametes and x_1,x_2,.......x_n

represent their proportions in the population $f_1 = \dfrac{x_i}{\sum\limits_{j=1^x j}^{n}}$ is the frequency

of a_1 in the population;

$i = 1, 2, 3,$.............n. $\sum\limits_{i=1}^{n} x_i a_i$ is called a state vector. Two states factors

$\sum\limits_{i=l}^{n} x_i a_i$ and $\sum\limits_{i=1}^{n} y_i a_i$ are equivalent if $\dfrac{x_i}{v_i} = r$; 1, 2,......n, $r > 0$ is real number

independent of i. A non empty subset k of a vector space A is called a cone without originif it is the closed under addition and multiplication by strictly positive scalers and k Ç (– k) = f. A cone K (S) is called polyhedral if it is the intersection of all cones which contain given finite subset Sof vectors. Define an equivalence ~ in A by $x \sim y$ if $x = ry$ for some $r > 0$. A ray in the linear space A is an equivalence class of the vectors of A. Here we are concerned with the polyhedral cone K K ({a_1,

$$a_2, \ldots\ldots, a_k\}) = \mathrm{K}(a_k) = \{x : xx \sum_{i=1}^{n} x_i a_i, x_i' s \geq 0, x \neq 0\}.$$

There is one-one correspondence between the rays in this cone and the state vectors representin states of a population. By random union of gamets of a_i and a_j zygotes of type $a_i a_j$ are formed, $i, j = 1,2, 3,\ldots\ldots,n$. Assume that a zygote $a_i a_j$ produces a number λ_{ijk} of gametes of type a_k of which $w_{ij}\ \lambda_{ijk}$ survive to reproduces.

This fact is expressed by the formal expression

$$a_{ij} = \sum_{k=1}^{n} w_{ij}\ \lambda i_{jk}\ a_k \qquad \ldots(1)$$

where w_{ij} is called visabilities. The $n \times n$ matrix (w_{ij}) is known as viability matrix. $1 - w_{ij}$ are called selection coefficients : $i, j = 1, 2, \ldots\ldots n$. If (1) is taken as the rule of multiplication of the basis elements in the vector space A and it is bilinearly extended onto A × A, then A becomes a non-associative algebra. It will be called a gametic algebra (with selection). A non-associative algebra over the vector space A is called conic if it admits a cone K which is closed under multiplication KK <K (vide Ringwood [25]). It is clear that the gametic algebra (with selection) described above is conic algebra. Since it admits a cone K (a_k) which is closed under multiplication. In what follows two state vectors $x = \Sigma x_i a_i$ and $y = \Sigma y_i a_i$ will be said to be equal if and only if they are equivalent i.e. $x = y \Leftrightarrow x \sim y$ i.e. $x_i = ry_i$ for real $r > 0$.

Clearly x will correspond to an equilibrium state if it is an indempotent ($x^2 = x$) in conic algebra A.

2. Selection Against Recessives

Consider the inheritance of a large random mating population with respect to two alleles a_1 and a_2 at a single locus, where a_1 is dominant and a_2 recessive. We have three genotypes $a_1\, a_1$, $a_1 a_2$, $a_2\, a_2$ called dominant, hybrid and recessive respectively. Since we are concerned with diploid population, We denote the gamete containing a_1 and a_2 by the same symbols. If x_1 and x_2 are proportions of a_1 and a_2 the state of the population can be representedby $x = x_1 a_1 + x_2 a_2$ initialy and by

$x^{(n)} = x_1^{(n)}a_1 + x_2^{(n)}a_2$ in the nth generation,

where $x^{(1)} = x^2$; $x^{(i)} = x^{(i-1)}(i-1)$; $\dfrac{x_1^{(n)}}{x_2^{(n)}} = u_n$ is the ratio of the allele frequencies. $u = \dfrac{x_1}{x_2}$ correspondence to initial generation. Now we can prove the following :

Theorem 1 : Consider two alleles a_1 and a_2 at a locus with proportions $x_1^{(n)}$ and $x_2^{(n)}$ respectively in the nth generation of a random mating population under selection against recessives and let $\dfrac{x_1^{(n)}}{x_2^{(n)}} = U_n$.

Then for real a, b, $\dfrac{\alpha}{u_n + \beta}$ can be expressed as a sum of 2^n fractions of the form $\dfrac{r}{u+\delta}$ where r. f are real numbers depending only upon the vability (or selection coefficient) and u is the initial values of u_n.

Proof : Assume that only a fraction w $(0 < w < 1)$ of the recessive a_2a_2 survive. Represent the initial state of the population by

$x = x_1a_1 + x_2a_2$; which is an element of a conic algebra A in which the multiplication is defined by the following table :

	a_1	a_2
a_1	a_1	$\frac{1}{2}(a_1 + a_2)$
a_2	$\frac{1}{2}(a_1 + a_2)$	wa_2

Clearly, $(x_1^2 + x_1x_2)a_1 + (x_2^2 w + x_1x_2)a_2 = x^2$

Let $rx_1^{(1)} = (x_1^2 + x_1x_2)$ ...(1)

and $rx_2^{(1)} = (wx_2^2 + x_1x_2)$ ...(2)

Dividing (1) by (2), we get

$$u_1 = \frac{u^2 + u}{w + u}$$

74 In general

$$u_n = \frac{n_{n-1}^2 + n_{n-1}}{w + u_{n-1}} \qquad ..(3)$$

For real a, b we have

$$\frac{\alpha}{u_n + \beta} = \frac{\alpha_1}{u_{n-1} + \beta_1} + \frac{\alpha_2}{u_{n-1} + p_2}$$

where;

$$a_1 = \frac{(a+w)}{a-b}$$

$$b_1 = a$$

$$a_2 = \frac{b + w}{b - a} \qquad ...(4)$$

$$b_2 = -b$$

$$a = -\frac{(1+\beta) + \sqrt{(1+\beta)^2 - 4w\beta)}}{2}$$

$$b = -\frac{(1+\beta) - \sqrt{(1+\beta)^2 - 4w\beta)}}{2}$$

Since $(1 + b)^2 > 4\,wb$, for all real values of b, it follows that *a* and *b* are real and unequal. Therefore, a_1, b_1, μ_2 b2 are all real numers. Now the result follows by inducation.

Special cases :

(*i*) $n = 1$, b $= -1$, a $= 1$

$$\frac{1}{u_{1-1}} = \frac{\alpha_1}{u + \beta_1} + \frac{\beta_2}{u + \beta_2}$$

Where, $a_1 = \dfrac{1 + \sqrt{w}}{2}$,

$$b_1 = -\sqrt{w}$$

$$a_2 = \frac{1-\sqrt{w}}{2}$$

$$b_2 = \sqrt{w}$$

$(ii)\, n=2, a \;\; =1, b =-1$

$$\frac{1}{n_{2-1}} = \frac{\alpha_{11}}{u+\beta_{11}} + \frac{\alpha_{12}}{u+\beta_{12}} + \frac{\alpha_{21}}{u+\beta_{21}} + \frac{\alpha_{22}}{u+\beta_{22}}$$

where,
$$a_{11} = \frac{1+\sqrt{w}[-1-\sqrt{w}) + \sqrt{[(1-\sqrt{w})^2 + 4w^{3/2}) + 2w]}}{4\sqrt{[(1-\sqrt{w})^2 + 4w^{3/2}]}},$$

$$b_{11} = \frac{(1-\sqrt{w}) - [(1-\sqrt{w})^2 + 4w^{3/2}}{2}$$

$$a_{12} = \frac{(1+\sqrt{w}[1-\sqrt{w}) + \sqrt{(1-\sqrt{w})^2 + 4w^{3/2}) + 2w]}}{4\sqrt{[(1-\sqrt{w})^2 + 4w^{3/2}]}}$$

$$b_{12} = \frac{(1-\sqrt{w}) + \sqrt{[(1-\sqrt{w})^2 + 4w^{3/2}}}{2}$$

$$a_{21} = \frac{(1-\sqrt{w}[-(-1-\sqrt{w}) + \sqrt{[(1-w)^2 + 4w^{3/4}) + 2w]}}{4\sqrt{[(1-w)^2 + 4w^{3/2})}}$$

$$b_{21} = \frac{(1-\sqrt{w}) - \sqrt{[(1-\sqrt{w})^2 + 4w^{3/2})}}{2}$$

$$\mu_{22} = \frac{(1-\sqrt{w}[1-\sqrt{w}) + \sqrt{[(1-\sqrt{w})^2 + 4w^{3/2}) + 2w]}}{4\sqrt{[(1-\sqrt{w})^2 + 4w^{3/2}}}$$

$$b_{22} = \frac{(1-\sqrt{w}) + \sqrt{(1-\sqrt{w})^2 + 4w^{3/2}}}{2}.$$

2.2. Selection Against Recessive with Mutation

Consider a large random mating population in which in generation a fraction p $(0<p<1)$ of a_1 allele mutate to a_2, a fraction q $(0<q<1)$ of a_2 allele mutate to a_1. Let the viability of the recessives a_2a_2 be w $(0<w<1)$.

Theorem-II : Let there be a large random mating population under the joint effect of mutation and selection againt recessive genotypes. If there are two alleles a_1 and a_2 is proportions $x_1^{(n)}$ and $x_2^{(n)}$ respectively in the nth generation and $\frac{x_1^{(n)}}{x_2^{(n)}} = u_n$, then for real a, b and $\frac{\alpha}{u_n+\beta}$ can be expressed as a sum of a real const.

m and 2^n fractious of the form $\frac{r}{u+\delta}$ where, rd are real numbers depending upon mutation rates and viability.

Proof : Represent the initial state of the population by $x = x_1a_1 + x_2a_2$: which is an element of a conic algebra A in which the multiplication i defined by the following table :

	a_1	a_2
a_1	$(1-p)\,a_1+pa_2$	$1/2\,[(1-p^+q)a_1+(1-q+p)a_2]$
a_2	$1/2\,[(1-p^+q)\,a_1+(1-q+p)\,a_2]$	$w\,[qa_1+(1-q)a_2]$

Clearly we have, $x^2 = x_x^{(1)}a_1 + x_2^{(1)}a_2$

Where $rx_1^{(1)} = x_1^2(1-p)+wqx_2^2+[(1-p)+q]x_1x_2$ ...(1)

$$rx_2^{(1)} = px_1^2+(p^+1-q)x_1x_2+w(1-q)x_2^2 \quad ...(2)$$

Dividing (1) by (2), we get

$$u_1 = \frac{u^2(1-p)+(1-p^+q)+w}{pu^2+(p^+1-q)u^+w(1-q)}$$

where $u_1 = \frac{x_1^{(1)}}{x_2^{(1)}};\ u = \frac{x_1}{x_2}$.

If $u_n = \frac{x_1^{(n)}}{x_2^{(n)}}$, then

$$\frac{\alpha}{u_n + \beta} = \frac{\alpha\,[pu_{n-1}^2 + (p^{+1-q})u_{n-1} + (1-q)w]}{(\beta p^{v1-p})n_{n-1}^2[(1-p+q+(p+1-q)\beta]u_{n-1} + wq + (1-q)w\beta}$$

Let $\quad s = \mathrm{b}p + 1 - p,$

$$t = q + (1-q)\beta,$$

then the discriminant of the denominator

$= (s+t)^2 - 4stw > 0$, independently of the real b, since $0 < w < 1$.

Hence $\quad \dfrac{\alpha}{u_n + \beta} = r_1 + \dfrac{\alpha_1}{u_{n-1} + \beta_1} + \dfrac{\alpha_2}{u_{n-1} + \beta_2}$

Where μ_1, b_1, a_2, b_2 are real numbers depending upon p, q, w. How the result follows by inducation.

Special case :

(*i*) When $n = 1, \mathrm{b} = 1, \mathrm{a} = 1,$

then $\quad \dfrac{1}{u_{1-1}} = p + \dfrac{\alpha_1}{u + \beta_1} + \dfrac{\alpha_2}{u + \beta_2}$

where,

$$\mathrm{a}_1 = \frac{(1-p-q)-1+\sqrt{(1-w)-\dfrac{w}{p}}}{2\sqrt{(1-w)}}$$

$$\mathrm{b}_1 = -1 + \sqrt{(1-w)}$$

$$\mathrm{a}_2 = \frac{(1-p-q)(1+\sqrt{(1-w)} + \dfrac{w}{p}}{2\sqrt{(1-w)}}$$

$$\mathrm{b}_2 = -\ 1 - 1\sqrt{(1-w)}$$

2.3. Three Alleles at a Locus with Selection against a Homozygous

Let us consider three alleles a_1, a_2, a_3 at a locus. Let the viability of the genotype a_3a_3 be w and that of all other genotypes be 1. How we can prove the following :

Theorem-III : Let there be three alleles a_1, a_2, a_3 at a locus and the selection be against only one homozygous, say a_3a_3. Let x_1, x_2, x_3 be their initial proportions and those $x_1^{(n)}, x_2^{(n)}, x_3^{(n)}$ in the nth generation, Assume

$$u_n = \frac{x_1^{(n)}}{x_3^{(n)}} + \frac{x_2^{(n)}}{x_3^{(n)}} \quad ; \quad u = \frac{x_1}{x_3} + \frac{x_2}{x_3}$$

$$v_n = \frac{x_1^{(n)}}{x_3^{(n)}} - \frac{x_2^{(n)}}{x_3^{(n)}} \quad ; \quad v = \frac{x_1}{x_3} - \frac{x_1}{x_3}$$

then for real a, b, $\frac{\alpha}{u_n + \beta}$ can be expressed as a sumof 2^n fractions of the form $\frac{r}{u+\delta}$ were r, d are real numbers depending upon the viability and v_n can be obtained by $\frac{u_n}{v_n} = \frac{u}{v}$.

Proof : Represent the initial state of the population by $x_1a_1 + x_2a_2 + x_3a_3$ which is an element of conic algebra in which multiplication is defined by the following table :

	a_1	a_2	a_3
a_1	a_1	$1/2\ (a_2 + a_3)$	$1/2\ (a_1 + a_3)$
a_2	$1/2\ (a_1 + a_2)$	a_2	$1/2\ (a_2 + a_3)$
a_3	$1/2\ (a_1 + a_3)$	$1/2\ (a_2 + a_3)$	wa^3

Clearly we have,

$$x^2 = x_1^{(1)}a_1 + x_2^{(1)}a_2 + x_3^{(1)}a_3$$

where,

$$rx_1^{(1)} = x_1^2 + x_1x_2 + x_1x_3$$

$$rx_2^{(1)} = x_1x_2 + x_2^2\ x_2x_3$$

$$rx_3^{(1)} = x_2x_3 + x_1x_3 + wx_3^2$$

Hence $$u_1 = \frac{u(u+1)}{u+w}$$

$$v_1 = \frac{v(u+1)}{u+w}$$

In general $$u_n = \frac{u_{n-1}(u_{n-1}+1)}{u_{n-1}+w} \quad ...(1)$$

$$v_n = \frac{v_{n-1}(w_{n-1}+1)}{v_{n-1}+w} \quad ...(2)$$

The form of the equation (1) is the same as the form of equation (3) of theorem 1. Hence it follows tht for real $\alpha, \beta, \frac{\alpha}{u_n+\beta}$ can be expressed as a sum of 2^n fraction of the form $\frac{r}{u+\delta}$ where r, d are real numbers depending upon w.

Also dividing (1) by (2), we get

$$\frac{u_n}{v_n} = \frac{u_{n-1}}{v_{n-1}}$$

i.e. $$\frac{u_n}{v_n} = \frac{u}{v} \quad ...(3)$$

from equation (3) v_n can be obtained.

Remark : The contents of this Chapter have been sent for publication in 'Mathematical Forum' (22).

Chapter-4

GAMETIC ALGEBRA OF TETRAPLOIDY UNDER SELECTION

4.1 Inheritance of Tetrapoloidy with Selection

Inheritance for polyploidy has been described by non-associative algebra by several authors [4, 6, 8, – 10, 14, 15, 17, 27, 31) in absence of selection. In this and the next chapter we describe the inheritance of tetraploidy and hexaploidy under selection by the use of algebra and basic idea of modern analysis.

In this chapter we consider an infinite random mating population of tetraploid individual which differ in a single locus with two alleles a_1, a_2. The 2-ploid gametes produced by the population are a_1a_1, a_1a_2 ($= a_2a_1$), a_2a_2 which will abbreviated as a_{11}, a_{12}, a_{22} in absence of selection the segregation behaviour of the gametest is given by the following table :

	a_{11}	a_{12}	a_{22}
a_{11}	a_{11}	$\frac{1}{2}(a_{11} + a_{12})$	$\frac{1}{6}a_{11} + \frac{2}{3}a_{12} + \frac{1}{6}a_{22}$
a_{12}		$\frac{1}{6}a_{11} + \frac{2}{3}a_{12} + \frac{1}{6}a_{22}$	$\frac{1}{2}(a_{12} + a_{22})$
a_{22}			a_{22}

In presence of selection the segregation behaviour of the gametes is given by following table (0 £ w_{ij} £ 1)

	a_{11}	a_{12}	a_{22}
a_{11}	$w_{11}a_{11}$	$\frac{1}{2}w_{12}(a_{11} + a_{12})$	$w_{13}(\frac{1}{6}a_{11} + \frac{2}{3}a_{12} + \frac{1}{6}a_{22})$
a_{12}	$\frac{1}{2}w_{21}(a_{11} + a_{12})$	$w_{22}(\frac{1}{6}a_{11} + \frac{2}{3}a_{12} + \frac{1}{6}a_{22})$	$\frac{1}{2}w_{23}(a_{12} + a_{22})$
a_{22}	$w_{31}(\frac{1}{6}a_{11} + \frac{2}{3}a_{12} + \frac{1}{6}a_{22})$	$\frac{1}{2}w_{32}(a_{12} + a_{22})$	$w_{33}\,a_{22}$

Table-2

Remarks : If the segregation behaviour is symetric i.e.

$$a_{ij}a_{k} = a_{kt}\, a_{ij}$$

then we assume

$$w_{ij} = w_{ji}$$

2. If we assume that (1) zygotes (union of two zygotes) containing same alleles have some segregation behaviour.

(II) If the alleles are interchanged, then the segregation behaviour of zygotes remain unchanged then,

$$w_{11} = w_{33} = w_1$$
$$w_{21} = w_{12} = w_{23} = w_{32} = w_2$$
$$w_{13} = w_{31} = w_{22} = w_3$$

4.2. The Evoluation Equation :

We assume that

$$w_{ij} = w_{ji}$$

Let $x = x_1a_{11} + x_2a_{12} + x_3a_{22}$

represent the state of a population in the initial generation.

The state of the population in the next generation is given by

$$x^2 = (x_1a_{11} + x_2a_{12} + x_3a_{22})^2$$

$$= x_1^2\, a_{11}^2 + x_2^2\, a_{12}^2 + x_3^2\, a_{22}^2 + 2x,x_2\, a_{11}\, a_{12} + 2x_1x_3\, a_{11}\, a_{22} + 2x_2\, x_3\, a_{12}\, a_{22}$$

$$x^2 = x_1^2\, w_{11}a_{11} + x_2^2\, w_{22}(\frac{1}{6}a_{11} + \frac{2}{3}a_{12} + \frac{1}{6}a_{22}) + x_3^2\, w_{33}\, a_{22} + x_1x_2w_{12}$$

$$+ (a_{11} + a_{12}) + 2x_1x_3w_{13}\left(\frac{1}{6}a_{11} + \frac{2}{3}a_{12} + \frac{1}{6}a_{22}\right) + x_2x_3w_{23}\,(a_{12} + a_{22})$$

$$= (x_1^2w_{11} + \frac{1}{6}x_2^2\, w_{22} + x_1w_{22} + \frac{1}{3}x_1x_3w_{13})\,a_{11}$$

$$+ (\frac{2}{3}x_2^2\, w_{22} + x_1x_2w_{12} + \frac{4}{3}x_1x_3w_{13} + x_2x_3w_{23})\,a_{12}$$

$$+ (\frac{1}{6}x_2^2\, w_{22} + x_3^2\, w_{33} + \frac{1}{3}x_1x_3w_{13} + x_2x_3w_{23})\,a_{22} \qquad ...(1)$$

If $x_1 + x_2 + x_3 = 1$, then the equation in normalized form is

$$\frac{x^2}{\| x^2 \|} = \frac{1}{w}[x_1^2 w_{11} + \frac{1}{6}x_2^2 w_{22} + x_1 x_2 w_{12} + \frac{1}{3}x_1 x_3 w_{13}]a_{11}$$

$$+ \left(\frac{2}{3}x_2^2 w_{22} + x_1 x_2 w_{12} + \frac{4}{3}x_1 x_3 w_{13} + x_2 x_3 w_{23}\right)a_{12}$$

$$+ (\frac{1}{6}x_2^2 w_{22} + x_3^2 w_{33} + \frac{1}{3}x_1 x_3 w_{13} + x_2 x_3 w_{23})a_{22}] \qquad ...(2)$$

Where,

$$\| x^2 \| \ w = x_1^2 w_{11} + x_2^2 w_{22} + x_3^2 w_{33} + 2x_2 x_3 w_{23} + 2x_3 x_1 w_{13} + 2x_1 x_2 w_{12}$$

4.3. Simplication of the Evolution Equation

In absence of selection (i.e., $w_{ij} = 1$) it is known that the evolution equation is greatly simplified if we change the basis (a_{11}, a_{12}, a_{22}) □ (c_0, c_1, c_2) by the self inverse transformation

$$c_0 = a_{11}$$
$$c_1 = a_{11} - a_{12}$$
$$c_2 = a_{11} - 2a_{12} + a_{22} \qquad ...(3)$$

Hence we obtain the equation reduced by the transformation (3) in same special cases :

Case-I : $w_{11} = 1 - s_1;$

$w_{33} = 1 - s_2;$

$w_{ij} = 1$ if ij □ 11, 33

We assume that $x_1 + x_2 + x_3 = 1$ then the equation (2) is

$$x^2 = \frac{1}{w}[(1-s_1)x_1^2 + \frac{1}{6}x_2^2 + x_1 x_2 + \frac{1}{3}x_1 x_3)a_{11} + (\frac{2}{3}x_2^2 + x_1 x_2$$

$$+ \frac{4}{3}x_1 x_3 + x_2 x_3)a_{12} + (\frac{1}{5}x_2^2 + \frac{1}{3}x_1 x_3 + x_2 x_3 + (1-s_2)x_3^2 a_{22}]$$

where $= (x_1 + x_2 + x_3)^2 - s_1 x_1^2 - s_2 x_3^2 = 1 - s_1 x_1^2 - s_2 x_3^2$

The equation in the normalized form is

$$\frac{x^2}{\| x^2 \|} = \frac{1}{w}(c_0 - y_1 c_1 + y_2 c_2)^2$$

where $y_1 = x_2 + 2x_3$

$y_2 = x_3$

$x_1 + x_2 + x_3 = 1$

From the table 2, we construct the following table for the composition of c_0, c_1, c_2.

	c_0	c_1	c_2
c_0	$(1-s_1)\,c_0$	$-\,s_1c_0+\frac{1}{2}c_1$	$-s_1c_0+\frac{1}{6}c_2$
c_1		$-s_1c_0+\frac{1}{6}c_2$	$-\,s_1c_0$
c_2			$-\,s_1c_0-s_2\,(c_0-2c_1+c_2)$

Table-3

Now, $$\frac{x^2}{\|x^2\|} = \frac{1}{w}[(c_0-y_1c_1)^2+2(c_0-y_1c_1)y_2c_2+y_2^2c_2^2]$$

$$= \frac{1}{w}[c_0^2-2y_1c_0c_1+y_1^2c_1^2+2y_2c_0c_2-2y_1y_2c_1c_2+y_2^2c_2^2]$$

$$= \frac{1}{w}[(1-s_1)c_0-2(-c_0s_1+c_1)y_1+(-s_1c_0+\frac{1}{6}c_2)y_1^2$$

$$+\ 2(-s_1c_0+\frac{1}{6}c_2)y_2-2(-s_1-s_1c_0)y_1y_2$$

$$+\ \{-s_1c_0-s_2(c_0-2c_1+c_2)y_2^2\}$$

$$= \frac{1}{w}[c_0-s_1c_0+2c_0s_1y_1-s_1c_0y_2^2-s_2c_0y_2^2-s_1c_0y_1^2$$

$$-\ 2s_1c_0y_2+2s_1c_0y_1y_2-2c_1y_1+2w_2c_1y_2^2$$

$$+\ \frac{1}{6}c_2y_1^2+\frac{2}{6}c_2y_2-s_2c_2y_2^2]$$

$$= \frac{1}{w}[(1-s_1+2s_1y_1-s_1y_2^2-s_2y_2^2-s_1y_1^2\ \ 2s_1y_2$$

$$+2s_1y_1y_2)c_0-(2y_1-2s_2y_2^2)c_1+(\frac{1}{6}+(\frac{1}{6}y_1^2+\frac{1}{3}y_2-s_2y_2^2)c_2]$$

$$=c_0-\frac{1}{w}(2y_1-2s_2y_2^2)\,c_1+\frac{1}{w}(\frac{1}{6}y_1^2+\frac{1}{3}y_2-s_2y_2^2)c_2$$

Hence, the reduced normalized equation in coordinat form is

$$y_1^1=\frac{1}{w}(2y_1-2s_2\,y_2^2)$$

$$=y_2^1=\frac{1}{w}(\frac{1}{6}y_1^2+\frac{1}{3}y_2-s_2\,y_2^2) \qquad ...(4)$$

Where, $w=1-s_1(1-y_1+y_2)^2-s_2y_2^2$

Case-II : Zygotes containing same alleles have same segregation behaviour and if the alleles are interchanged then the segregation behaviour of zygote remains unchanged.

i.e. $w_{11}=w_{33}=w_1$

$w_{21}=w_{12}=w_{23}=w_{32}=w_2$

$w_{13}=w_{31}=w_{22}=w_2$

The multiplication table is :

	a_{11}	a_{12}	a_{22}
a_{11}	w_1a_{11}	$\frac{1}{2}w_2(a_{11}+a_{12})$	$w_3(\frac{1}{6}a_{11}+\frac{2}{3}a_{12}$ $+\frac{1}{6}a_{22}$
a_{12}	$\frac{1}{2}w_2(a_{11}+a_{12})$	$w_3(\frac{1}{6}a_{11}+\frac{2}{3}a_{12}$ $+\frac{1}{6}a_{22})$	$\frac{1}{2}w_2(a_{12}+a_{22})$
a_{22}	$w_3(\frac{1}{6}a_{11}+\frac{2}{3}a_{12}$ $+\frac{1}{6}a_{22})$	$\frac{1}{2}w_2(a_{12}+a_{22})$	w_1a_{22}

Table-4

In this case transformation (3) does not help in the reduction of equation (2). Hence we seek a general transformation of the basis in the form :

$$c_0 = a_{11}$$
$$c_1 = ka_{11} - a_{12}$$
$$c_2 = k_1 a_{11} - k_2 a_{12} + a_{22}$$

which has the inverse

$$a_{11} = c_0$$
$$a_{12} = -(k_1 + k_2\, x)c_0 + k_2 c_1 + c_2$$
$$a_{22} = c_2 - k_1$$

$$c_0 c_1 = w_1 k\, a_{11} - \frac{w_2}{2}(a_{11} + a_{12})$$

$$= (kw_1 - \frac{w_2}{2})a_{11} - \frac{w_2}{2}a_{12}$$

$$= \frac{w_2}{2}[(\frac{2kw_1}{w_2} - 1)a_{11} - a_{12}]$$

Choose k such that

$$\frac{2kw_1}{w_2} - 1 = k$$

$$k(\frac{2w_1}{w_2} - 1) = 1$$

\ $$k = \frac{w_2}{2w_1 - w_2}$$

$$c_0 c_2 = k_1 a_{11}^2 + k_2 a_{11} a_{12} + a_{11} a_{22}$$

$$= kw_1 a_{11} + k_2 1/2\, w_2(a_{11} + a_{12}) + w_3(\frac{1}{6}a_{11} + \frac{2}{3}a_{12} + \frac{1}{2}a_{22})$$

$$= (k_1 w_1 + \frac{1}{2}k_2 w_2 + \frac{1}{6}w_3)a_{11} + (\frac{1}{2}k_2 w_2 + \frac{2}{3}w_3)a_{12} + \frac{1}{6}w_3\, a_{22}$$

$$c_0c_2 = (k_1w_1 + \frac{1}{2}k_2w_2 + \frac{1}{6}w_3)c_0 + (\frac{1}{2}k_2w_2 + \frac{2}{3}w_3)(kc_0 - c_1)$$

$$+ \frac{1}{6}w_3\{(-(k_1 + k_2k)c_0 + k_2c_1 + c_2)\}$$

$$c_0c_2 = [k_1w_1 + \frac{1}{2}k_2w_2 + \frac{1}{6}w_3 1 - (k_1 + k_2k)]c_0$$

$$+[-(\frac{1}{2}k_2w_2 + \frac{2}{3}w_3) + \frac{1}{6}k_2w_3]c_1 + \frac{1}{6}w_3c_2$$

Now we choose k_1 and k_2 such that

$$k_1w_1 + \frac{1}{2}k_2w_2 + \frac{1}{6}w_3\{1 - (k_1 + kk_2)\} = 0 - (\frac{1}{2}k_2w_2 + \frac{2}{3}w_3) + \frac{1}{6}k_2w_3 = 0$$

\ $$k_2 = \frac{4w_3}{3w_2 - w_3}$$

$$k_1 = \frac{w_3(9w_2 + w_3)}{(3w_2 - w_3)(6w_1 - w_3)}$$

Hence the transformation is

$$c_0 = a_{11}$$

$$c_1 = \frac{w_2}{2w_1 - w_2}a_{11} - a_{12}$$

$$c_2 = \frac{w_3(9w_2 + w_3)}{(3w_2 - w_3)(6w_1 - w_3)}a_{11} - \frac{4w_3}{3w_2 - w_3}a_{12} - a_{22} \qquad ...(5)$$

The inverse is

$$a_{11} = c_0$$

$$a_{12} = \frac{w_2}{2w_1 - w_2}c_0 - c_1$$

$$a_{22} = \frac{w_3(3w_2 + 2w_2)}{(2w_1 - w_2)(6w_1 - w_3)}c_0 - \frac{4w_3}{2w_2 - w_3}c_1 + c_2 \qquad ...(6)$$

How the new multiplication table is :

	c_0	c_1	c_2
c_0	$w_1 c_0$	$\frac{1}{2} w_2 c_1$	$\frac{1}{6} w_3 c_2$
c_1		$1_0 c_0 + 1_1 e_1 + 1_2 c_2$	$m_0 c_0 + m_1 c_1 + m_2 c_2$
c_2			$n_0 c_0 + n_1 c_1 + n_2 c_2$

Table-5

Remarks : 1. In the above 1's, m's, n's are rational functions of w_1, w_2, w_3.

2. The trans (5) and (6) are free from singularities only if $2w_1$ □ w_2, $6w_1$ □ w_3, $3w_2$ □ w_3.

3. If $w_1 = w_2 = w_3$, then (5) reduces to (3).

Reduction of the equation (1)

Let, $x = x_1 a_{11} + x_2 a_{11} + a_{22}$, be the initial state of the population.

Then $$x = x_1 c_0 + x_2 [\frac{w_2}{2w_1 w_2} c_0 - c_1]$$

$$+ [\frac{w_3(3w_2 + 2w_3)}{(2w_1 - w_2)(6w_1 - w_2)} c_0 - \frac{4w_3}{3w_2 - w_3} c_1 + c_2]$$

$= y_0 c_0 + y_1 c_1 + c_2$, from the equation (5).

where

$$y_0 = x_1 + \frac{w_2}{2w_1 - w_2} x_2 + \frac{w_3(3w_2 + 2w_3)}{(2w_1 - w_2)(6w_1 - w_3)}$$

$$y_1 = -x_2 - \frac{4w_3}{3w_2 - w_3}$$

\ $x^2 = \frac{1}{k}(y_0 c_0 + y_1 c_1 + c_2)^2$, where k is the coefficient of c_2 in the expansion of $(y_0 c_0 + y_1 c_1 + y_2 c_2)^2$

$$= \frac{1}{k}(y_0^2 c_0^2 + y_1^2 c_1^2 + c_2^2 + 2y_0 y_1 c_0 y_1 + 2y_1 c_1 c_2 + 2y_0 c_0 y_2)$$

$$= \frac{1}{k}[(w_1 y_0^2 + 1_0 y_1^2 + n_0 + 2y_1 m_0)c_0$$

$$+(y_1^2 1_1 + n_1 + y_0 y_1 w_2 + 2n_1 y_1)c_1 + (y_1^2 1_2 + n_2 + 2n_2 y_1 + \frac{1}{3} y_0 w_3)c_2]$$

$$= \frac{w_1 y_0^2 + 1_0 y_1^2 + 2y_1 n_0 + n_0}{\frac{1}{2} w_3 y_0 + k_2 y_1^2 + 2n_2 y_1 + n_2} c_0 + \frac{y_1^2 1_1 + y_1(y_0 w_2 + 2n_1) + n_1}{\frac{1}{3} w_3 y_0 + 1_2 y_1^2 + 2n_2 y_1 + n_2} c_1 + c_2$$

Remark : The above equation is not in the normalized form.

4.4. Equilibria of the Tetraploid Population

Equilibrium states of a tetraploid populations correspond to the idempotents in the algebra which describe the inheritance of the population clearly the idempotents are the fixed points of the evolution transformation defined by the evolution equation. The genetic interpretation of the equilibria is that allelic and genetypic frequencies of a population is equilibrium remains the same in every generation. Further in absence of selection it is show that in several real genetic situation of the population tends to an equilibrium state. (Vide Goshor [8-9], Worz-Busekras [31].

In this chapter we fixed equilibria of the polyploid population by obtaining idempotents in the algebra or by obtaining fixed points of the evolution transformation using Brouwer's fixed point theorem. Brouwer's theorem states that any continuous mapping of a bounded, convex, closed set into itself has fixed point.The equilibra will be obtained under the assumption that the zygotes containing same alleles have identical segregation behaviour and the segregation behaviour of a zygote remain unchanged if the alleles are interchanged. Idempotents in the algebra is given by

$$(x_1 a_{11} + x_2 a_{12} + x_3 a_{22})^2 = (x_1 a_{11} + x_2 a_{12} + x_3 a_{22})$$

or

$$(w_1 x_1^2 + \frac{1}{6} w_3 x_2^2 + x_1 x_2 w_2 + \frac{1}{3} x_1 x_3 w_3) a_{11}$$

$$+(\frac{2}{3} x_2^2 w_3 + x_1 x_2 w_2 + x_2 x_3 w_2 + \frac{4}{3} x_1 x_3 w_3) a_{12}$$

$$+ (\frac{1}{6} x_2^2 w_2 + w_1 x_3^2 + x_2 x_3 w_2 + \frac{1}{3} x_1 x_3 w_3) a_{22}$$

$$= x_1a_{11} + x_2a_{12} + x_3a_{22}$$

$$w_1x_1^2 + \frac{1}{6}w_3x_2^2 + x_1x_2w_2 + \frac{1}{3}x_1x_3w_3 = x_1 \quad ...(1)$$

$$\frac{2}{3}x_2^2w_3 + x_1x_2w_2 + x_2x_3w_2 + \frac{4}{3}x_1x_3w_3 = x_2 \quad ...(2)$$

$$\frac{1}{6}x_2^2\,w_3 + w_1x_3^2 + x_2x_3w_2 + \frac{1}{3}x_1x_3w_3 = x_3 \quad ...(3)$$

Substracting equation (3) from (1)

$$w_1x_1^2 + x_1x_2w_2 - w_1x_3^2 - x_2x_3w_2 = x_1 - x_3$$

i.e. $(x_1 - x_3)\,(w_1x_1 + x_3) + w_2x_2 - 1) = 0$

Hence, we consider the following two cases

4.4.1 case-1 $x_1 = x_3$; we prove the following theorem.

Theorem-I : In the algebra of tetraploid given by table 2, there is an indepotent of the form

$x_1a_{11} + x_2a_{12} + x_1a_{22}$, $2x_1 + x_2 = 1$; if $w_1, w_2, w_3\ 0$

Proof : The normalized evolution transformation

$f: x\frac{x^2}{\|x^2\|}$ given by

$$x\frac{x^2}{\|x^2\|} = \frac{1}{w}[(w_1x_1^2 + \frac{1}{6}w_3x_2^{2+} + x_1x_2w_2 + \frac{1}{3}x_1^2w_3)\,a_{11}$$

$$+(\frac{2}{3}x_2^2w_3 + x_1x_2w_2 + x_1x_2w_2 + \frac{4}{3}x_1^2\,w_3)a_{12}$$

$$+\ (\frac{1}{6}x_2^2\,w_3 \mid w_1x_1^2 + x_1x_2w_2 + \frac{1}{3}x_1^2\,w_3)\,a_{22}]$$

$$= x_1a_{11} + x_2a_{12} + x_1a_{22}$$

where $w = w_1x_1^2 + w_3x_2^2 + w_1x_1^2 + 4x_1x_2w_2 + 2x_1^2w_3$ clearly the coordinate functions

$$f_1(x_1, x_2, x_1) - \frac{1}{w}(w_1x_1^2 + \frac{1}{6}w_3x_2^? + w_2x_1x_2 + \frac{1}{3}w_3x_1^2)$$

$$x_1\ x_2\ x_1 = \frac{1}{w}(\frac{2}{3}w_3x_2^2 + w_2x_1x_2 + w_2x_1x_2 + \frac{4}{3}w_3x_1)$$

$$f_3(x_1, x_2, x_1) = f_1\ (x_1, x_2, x_1)$$

are continuous under the conditions of the theorem.

Hence the function f is continious.

Next we note that the domain

$D = \{(x_1, x_2, x_3) : x_1 - x_3 = 0, x_1 + x_2 + x_3 = 1, x_1, x_2, x_3 \square R\}$ is obtained by linear constrainsts on IR^3 and so it is convex.

Since $0 \pounds x, \pounds 1$, D is bounded.

To prove that D is closed.

It is sufficient to show that D^c is open.

Let, (x_1, x_2, x_1) D^c

and $$r = \frac{1}{2}[1-(2x_1 + x_2]$$

Consider the open sphere $S_r\ (x_1, x_2, x_1)$

If possible let $S_r\ (x_1, x_2, x_1)$

Contain $(x_1^1, x_2^1, x_1^1)\, \varepsilon\, D$ then

$$2(x_1 - x_1^1)^2 + \frac{1}{2}(x_2 - x_2^1)^2 + \frac{1}{2}(x_2 - x_2^1) < r^2$$

$$= \frac{1}{2}[4(x_1 - x_1^1)^2 + (x_2 - x_2^1)^2]\frac{1}{2}(x_2 - x_2^1) < r^2$$

$$= \frac{1}{2}[4(x_1 - x_1^1)^2 + (x_2 - x_2^1)^2] + \frac{1}{2}(x_2 - x_2^1) < r^2$$

$$\frac{1}{4}[1-(2x_1 + x_2)]^2 + (x_2 - x_2^1)^2 < \frac{1}{4}[1-(2x_1 + x_2)]^2$$

which is a contradictions

Hence Sr $(x_{11}, \mathrm{x}_2, x_1)$ contains no point of D.

Since (x_1, x_2, x_1) is arbitrary, it follows that D^c is open i.e. D is a closed set.

Hence, by Brouwer's fixed point theorem it follows that f has a fixed point which is an idempotent in the algebra. Hence the theorem.

By actual computation it is seen that the idempotent is $x_1a_{11} + x_2a_{12} + x_1a_{11}$ where x_1 is the root of the equation

$$\phi(x_1) = (\frac{1}{6}w_3w_1 - \frac{1}{4}w_1w_2^2 + \frac{1}{12}w_3w_2^2)x_1^3 + (\frac{1}{4}w_2^2 + \frac{1}{12}w_2w_3 - \frac{1}{3}w_1w_3)x_1^2$$

$$+ (\frac{1}{16}w_1 + \frac{3}{16}w_3)x_1 - \frac{1}{16} = 0 \qquad ...(4)$$

and x_2 is given by

$$x_2 = \frac{x_1 - w_1x_1^2}{\frac{1}{4} + \frac{1}{2}x_1w_2} \qquad ...(5)$$

The existence of the idempotent also follows the intermediate value theorem of the analysis, we note that ϕ is a continuous function and

$$\phi(0) = -\frac{1}{16} < 0.$$

$\phi(\frac{1}{w_1}) > 0$. Henc x_1 has a root in the interval $]\,0, \frac{1}{w_1}[$

For this value of x_1 by (5) $x_2 > 0$.

Finally we consider a special case when $x_1 = x_2 = x_3 = x_1$

By equation (1), (2) and (3), for $x_1 = x_2 = x_3$ we must have

$$w_1 + \frac{1}{6}w_3 + w_2 + \frac{1}{3}w_3 = \frac{2}{3}w_3 + 2w_2 + \frac{4}{3}w_3$$

i.e. $w_1 - w_2 = \frac{1}{6}(12w_3 - w_3 - 2w_3)$

$$w_1 - w_2 = \frac{3}{2}w_3$$

The condition is satisfied when

$$w_1 = 1,\ w_2 = \frac{1}{2}, w_3 = \frac{1}{3}.$$

The idempotent corresponds to $x = \frac{3}{5}$

4.42 Case-II : $w_1(x_1+x_3)+x_2w_2=1$

In this case the equations are

$$w_1x_1^2+\frac{1}{6}w_3x_2^2+x_1x_2w_3+\frac{1}{3}x_1x_3w_3= x_1[w_1(x_1+x_3)+x_2x_3] \quad ...(6)$$

$$\frac{2}{3}x_2^2\,w_3+x_1x_2w_2+x_2x_3w_3+\frac{4}{3}x_1x_3w_3 = x_2[w_1(x_1+x_3)+x_2w_2] \quad ...(7)$$

$$\frac{1}{6}w_3x_2^2+x_1x_3(\frac{1}{3}-w_1)=0 \quad ...(6^1)$$

$$(\frac{2}{3}w_3-w_2)x_2^2+(w_2-w_1)x_1x_2+(w_2-w_1)x_2x_3+\frac{4}{3}x_1x_3w_3 \quad (7^1)$$

The equilibrium point corresponds to a ray common to the two cones (6^1) and (7^1) and lying in the positive centant.

$$x_1x_3\frac{6w_1-2w_3}{w_3}\,(\frac{2}{3}w_3-w_2)+(w_2-w_1)(x_1+x_3)\frac{6w_1-2w_3}{w_3}x_1x_3$$

$$+\frac{4}{3}w_3x_1x_3=0$$

i.e. $$(w_2-w_1)\frac{6w_1-2w_3}{w_3}(x+\frac{1}{x})$$

$$+\left[\frac{(6w_1-2w_3)(\frac{2}{3}w_3-w_2)+\frac{4}{3}w_3^2}{w_3}\right]=0$$

where $x=\sqrt{\dfrac{x_1}{x_3}}$

i.e. $$(w_2-w_1)\sqrt{\frac{6w_1-2w_3}{w_3}}(x+\frac{1}{x})$$

$$+\frac{4w_1w_3-6w_1w_2-\frac{4}{3}w_3^2+2w_2w_3+\frac{4}{3}w_3^2}{w_3}=0$$

i.e. $(w_2 - w_1)\sqrt{w_3(6w_1 - 2w_3)}\,(x + \frac{1}{x}) + 4w_1w_3 + 6w_1w_2 + 2w_2w_2 = 0$

$$(x + \frac{1}{x})^2 = \frac{(4w_1w_3 - 6w_1w_2 + 2w_2w_3)^2}{(w_2 - w_1)^2 w_3(6w_1 - 2w_3)}$$

$$(y + \frac{1}{y}) = \frac{(4w_1w_3 - 6w_1w_2 + 2w_2w_3)^2}{(w_2 - w_1)^2 w_3(6w_1 - 2w_3)} - 2 \qquad ...(8)$$

where $y = \frac{x_1}{x_3}$

This is an equation to get $\frac{x_1}{x_3}$

The x_2 is obtained by equation (1)

$$\frac{1}{2}(y + \frac{1}{y}) = \frac{2(2w_1w_3 - 3w_1w_2 + w_2w_3)^2}{(w_2 - w_1)^2 w_3(3w_1 - w_3)} - 1 \qquad ...(9)$$

The solution of (9) is not possible for generalvalues of w_1, w_2, w_3. However, solution of (9) exist if

1. $3w_1 - w_3 > 0,\ w_1 \square w_2$
2. $2w_1w_3 - 3w_1w_2 + w_2w_3$

$$> |w_1 - w_2|\sqrt{w_3(3w_1 - w_3)}$$

An example of an idempotent satisfying the case-II is

$$(\frac{5 + 3\sqrt{2}}{12})a_{11} + \frac{7}{12}a_{12} + \frac{(5 - 3\sqrt{2})}{12}a_{22}$$

provided $w_1 = \frac{1}{2}, w_2 = 1, w_3 = \frac{1}{3}$.

This result is going to appear in JBMS. Vol. 14 [29].

4.5 Optimization of Gamete Frequencies in Tetraploid Population

In population gemetics one important problem is to maximize the frequency of a gamete containing beneficial genes or to minimize the frequency of a gemete having harmful genes in a population. Well-known practical method for this purpose is the artificial selection. Unfortunately a theoretical background to tackle such problems for the autopolypoid individuals is lacking in the literature. The history of mathematical genetics indicates that no one has taken up this problem in general framework. Here we pose the problem and forward solutions for the tetraploid (and hexaploid) populations. However the technique is quite general and can be extended to the population of r-ploid individuals with suitable modifications.

Optimization Problem for Gamete Frequency

Let x_1, x_2, be frequencies of the gametes a_1 a$_1$, a_1a_2 and a_2a_2 in a population of tetraploids. Let the inheritance of the population be given by the table-2 (Selection 4.1 then). Then (0 to 10 obtain the values of x_1,x_2m x_3 in initial generation such that it gives maximum (or minimum) values of the frequency $f(x_1)$ of a particular gamete, say a_1a_1 in the filial generation.

(0_2) To obtain the values of x_1, x_2, x_3 in initial generation such that it gives maximum (or minimum) values of the frequency $\mu_1^{(n)}$ of a particular gamete, say a_1a_1 in the nth generation.

(0_3) To obtain the asymptotic values of the frequency of a_1a_1.

(A) We shall exhibit a solution in the closed form of the problem(0_1), (0_2) and (0_3) under the following conditions.

I. Zygotes (union of two gametes) containing same alleles have ame segregation behaviour.

II. If the alleles are interchanged then the segragation behaviour of a zygote remains unchanged.

Condition (I) and (II) □

$$w_{12} = w_{21} = w_{23} = w_{32} = w_2$$
$$w_{11} = w_{33} = w_1$$
$$w_{13} = w_{31} = w_{22} = w_3$$

(III) $x_1 = x_3$

We do this in a series of theorems stated below :

Theorem-I

If (i) a root ± of the equation

$2(3w_1w_2 - 4w_1w_3 + w_2w_3)x^2 - 4w_3(w_2 - w_1)x^4w_2w_3 = 0$

$0 < w_1, w_2, w_3$ £ 1

belongs to the close interval [0, ½] and (*ii*)the root are unequal if the equation is quadratic,

$$\text{then max } f(x_1) = f(\pm),$$
$$\min f(x_1) = f(o)$$
$$\text{otherwise max } f(x_1) = f(1/2),$$
$$\min f(x_1) = f(o)$$
$$\text{where } f(o) = 1/6,$$

$$f\left(\frac{1}{2}\right) = \frac{w_1 + \frac{1}{3}w_3}{2(w_1 + w_3)}$$

$$f(x) = \frac{ax^2 + bx + c}{a_1x^2 + b_1x + c_1},$$

where

$$a = w_1 - 2w_2 + w_3$$

$$b = w_2 - \frac{2}{3}w_3$$

$$c = \frac{1}{6}w_3 \qquad \text{...(1)}$$

$$a_1 = 2w_1 - 8w_2 + 6w_3$$
$$b_1 = 4(w_2 - w_3)$$
$$c_1 = w_3$$

If $2w_2^3 \neq w_3^2 + w_1w_3$ and $3w_1w_2 - 4w_1w_2 + w_2w_3 \neq 0$ then $f(\pm)$ can be also give by

$$f(\pm) = \frac{-\frac{4}{3}\left(2w_1w_3 + w_3^2 - 3w_2^2\right) \pm \frac{2}{3}\sqrt{4w_1^2 w_3^2 + 2w_2^2 w_3^2 - 6w_1 w_2^2 w_3}}{8\left(2w_2^2 - w_3^2 - w_1w_3\right)}$$

where $f()$ corresponds to positive or negative sign of the square root according as ± corresponds to the positive or negative sign of the square root in the formula

$$= \frac{2w_3(w_2 - w_1) \pm \sqrt{2w_2^3 w_3^2 + 4w_1^2, w_3^2 - 6w_1 w_2^2 w_3}}{2\left(3w_1 w_2 - 4w_1 w_3 + w_2 w_3\right)}$$

Proof : The normalized evolution equation is

$$x_1^{(1)} a_{11} + x_2^{(1)} a_{12} + x_3^{(1)} a_{22} = \frac{x^2}{//x^2//}$$

$$= \frac{1}{W}\left[\begin{array}{l}\left(X_2^1 w_{11} + \frac{1}{6} x_2^2 w_{22} + x_1 x_2 w_{12} + \frac{1}{3} x_1 x_3 w_{13}\right) a_{11} \\ + \left(\frac{2}{3} x_2^2 w_{22} + x_1 x_2 w_{12} + \frac{4}{3} x_1 x_3 w_{13} + x_2 x_3 w_{23}\right) a_{12} \\ + \left(\frac{1}{6} x_2^2 w_{22} + x_3^2 w_{33} + \frac{1}{3} x_1 x_3 w_{13} + x_3 x_3 w_{23}\right) a_{22}\end{array}\right]$$

where

$$W = x_1^2 w_{11} + x_2^2 w_{22} + x_3^2 w_{33} + 2x_2 x_3 w_{23} + 2x_3 x_1 w_{13} + 2x_1 x_2 w_{12}$$

$a_1 a_1 = a_{11}, a_1 a_2 = a_{12}, a_2 a_2 = a_{22}$

In view of conditions I, II and III of the theorem the normalized evolution equation becomes

$$x_1^{(1)} a_{11} + x_2^{(1)} a_{12} + x_3^{(1)} a_{22}$$

$$= \frac{1}{w}\left[\begin{array}{l}\left(w_1 x_1^2 + \frac{1}{6} x_2^2 w_3 + x_1 x_2 w_2 + \frac{1}{3} x_1^2 w_3\right) a_{11} \\ + \left(\frac{2}{3} x_2^2 w_3 + 2x_1 x_2 w_2 + \frac{4}{3} x_1^2 w_3\right) a_{12} \\ + \left(\frac{1}{6} x_2^2 w_3 + w_1 x_1^2 + x_1 x_2 w_2 + \frac{1}{3} x_1^2 w_3\right) a_{22}\end{array}\right]$$

where

$$W = w_1 x_1^2 + w_3 x_2^2 + w_1 x_1^2 + 4x_1 x_2 w_2 + 2x_1^2 w_3,\ 2x_1 + x_2 = 1$$

and $a_1 a_1 = a_{11}, a_1 a_2 = a_{12}, a_2 a_2 = a_{22}$

Since $2x^{(1)} + x^{(2)} = 1$, it is sufficient to consider the maximum and minimum values

$$x_1^{(1)} = f(x_1)$$

$$= \frac{1}{w}\left[w_1 x_1^2 + \frac{1}{6} w_3 x_2^2 w_2 x_1 x_2 + \frac{1}{3} x_1^2 w_3\right]$$

Putting $x_2 = 1 - 2x_1$, we have $x_1^{(1)} = f(x_1) = \dfrac{ax_1^2 + bx_1 + c}{a_1x_1^2 + b_1x_1 + c_1}$

where a, b, c and a_1, b_1, c_1 are given in equal (1). For simplicity we write x in place of x_1.

Then we have to maximize or minimize

$$f(x) = \frac{ax^2 + bx + c}{a_1x^2 + b_1x + c_1} \qquad ...(2)$$

where $0 \le x \le \dfrac{1}{2}$

since $0 \le x \le \dfrac{1}{2} \Rightarrow 0 \le f(x) \le \dfrac{1}{2}$, f a continuous function defined on the closed and bounded (*i.e.*, compact) interval $\left[0, \dfrac{1}{2}\right]$ in R, P attains its maximum and minimum values in $\left[0, \dfrac{1}{2}\right]$. We have

$$f^1(x) = \frac{(ab_1 - a_1, b)x^2 - 2(ca_1 - c_1a)x + (bc_1 - b_1c)}{(a_1x^2 + b_1x + c_1)^2} \qquad ...(3)$$

where $\qquad f^1(x) = \dfrac{df(x)}{dx}$

$$ab_1 - a_1b = \frac{2}{3}(3w_1w_2 - 4w_1w_3 + w_2w_3) \qquad ...(4)$$

$$bc_1 - b_1c = \frac{1}{3}w_2w_3$$

$$ca_1 - c_1a = \frac{2}{3}w_3(w_2 - w_1)$$

We assume that

$$\Delta = 3w_1w_1 - 4w_1w_3 + w_2w_3 \ne 0 \qquad ...(5)$$

Let ✚ , ɞ be the root of the equation

$(ab_1 - a_1b)x^2 - 2(ca_1 - c_1a)x + (bc_1 - b_1c) = 0$

i.e. $2(3w_1w_2 - 4w_1w_3 + w_2w_3)x^2 - 4w_3(w_2 - w_1) + w_2w_3 = 0$ ...(6)

$0 < w_1, w_2 w_3 £ 1$

The discriminant of (5) is

$$D = 2w_2^2 w_3^2 + 4w_1^2 w_3^2 - 6w_1 w_2^2 w_3 \quad ...(7)$$

Now following cases arise :

Case I :

$$\alpha, \beta \square \left[0, \frac{1}{2}\right]$$

In this case $f^1(x) = \dfrac{\Delta(x-\alpha)(x-\beta)}{(a_1x^2 + b_1x + c)^2}$

We consider the following subscases :

Case I$_a$:

α and β are imaginary

Let, $\alpha = A + iB$

$\beta = A - iB$, where A and B are real numbers

first we show that $\Delta > 0$

α, β imaginary

$\square$ Discriminant ofthe equations (4) < 0

$\square \quad w_2^2 w_3^2 + 2w_1^2 < 2w_1 w_2^2 w_3$

$\square \quad w_3 < \dfrac{3w_1w_2^2}{w_2^2 + 2w_1^2}$

Now $\Delta = 3w_1w_2 - 4(w_1 - w_2)w_3$

$$> 3w_1 w_2 - \frac{(4w_1 - w_2)3w_1 w_2}{w_2^2 + 2w_1^2}$$

$$= \frac{6w_1 w_2(w_1 + w_2)^2}{w_2^2 + 2w_1^2} > 0$$

Now $f^1(x) = \dfrac{\Delta[x-(A+iB)][x-(A-iB)]}{\left(a_1x^2 + b_1x + c_1\right)^2}$

$$= \frac{\Delta\left[(x-A)^2 + B^2\right]}{\left(a_1x^2 + b_1x + c_1\right)^2} > 0$$

$f(x)$ is monotoric increasing in $\left[0, \frac{1}{2}\right]$

Hence max $f(x) = f\left(\frac{1}{2}\right)$

min $f(x) = f(0)$

where $x \in \left[0, \frac{1}{2}\right]$

Case I_b : $\alpha\beta < 0, \alpha$ □ β

From equation (4) we have

$$\alpha\beta = \frac{w_2 w_3}{2\Delta} \qquad ...(8)$$

□ $\Delta < 0$

Also $(x - \alpha)(x - \beta) < 0$ for $x \in \left[0, \frac{1}{2}\right]$

Hence $f^1(x) > 0$

i.e. $f^1(x)$ is monotonically increasing in $\left[0, \frac{1}{2}\right]$ and so

max $f(x_1) = f\left(\frac{1}{2}\right)$

min $f(x_1) - f(0)$

Case I_c :

$\alpha\beta > 0, \alpha$ □ β

From equation (4) we have

$$\alpha\beta = \frac{w_2 w_3}{2\Delta}$$

□ $\Delta > 0$ also $(x-\alpha)(x-\beta)\, 0$, for $x \notin \left[0, \frac{1}{2}\right]$

Hence $f^1(x) > 0$

i.e. $f^1(x)$ is monotonic increasing in $\left[0, \frac{1}{2}\right]$ and so

$$\max \quad f(x_1) = f\left(\frac{1}{2}\right),$$

$$\min \quad f(x_1) = f(0)$$

Case I_d:

$$\alpha = \beta$$

In this case discriminant D of the equation (4) vanishes i.e.

$$w_2^2 w_3^2 + 2w_1^2 w_3^2 = 3w_1 w_2^2 w_3$$

Then

$$\Delta = 3w_1 w_2 - (4w_1 - w_2) w_3$$

$$= 3w_1 w_2 - \frac{(4w_1 - w_2) 3w_1 w_2}{w_2^2 + 2w_1^2}$$

$$= \frac{6w_1 w_2 (w_1 + w_2)^2}{w_2^2 + 2w_1^2} > 0$$

Thus

$$f^1(x) = \frac{\Delta (x-\alpha)^2}{\left(a_1 x^2 + b_1 x + c_1\right)^2} > 0$$

Since $\alpha \notin [0, \frac{1}{2}]$

Hence

$$\max f(x) = f\left(\frac{1}{2}\right)$$

$$\min f(x) = f(0)$$

where $x \in \left[0, \frac{1}{2}\right]$

Case-II :

$$\alpha \in \left[0, \frac{1}{2}\right], \beta \notin \left[0, \frac{1}{2}\right]$$

In this case $\alpha > 0$, $\beta > 0$

$$\Rightarrow \quad \alpha\beta > 0 \quad \begin{cases} f^1(x) \le 0, \forall x \sum \left[a, \frac{1}{2}\right] \\ f^1(x) \ge 0, \forall x \in [0, \alpha] \end{cases}$$

$$\Rightarrow \quad \Delta > 0 \quad \Rightarrow$$

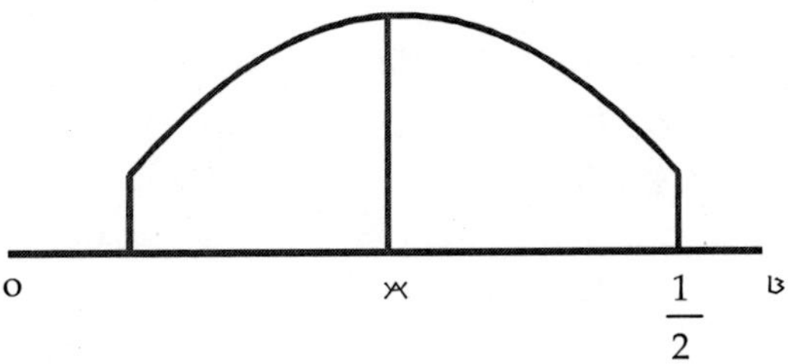

Hence max $\quad f(x) = f(\alpha)$

$$x \in [0, \alpha]$$

$$\max f(x) = f(\alpha)$$

$$x \in \left[\alpha, \frac{1}{2}\right]$$

Hence, $\quad \max f(x) = f(\alpha)$

$$\min f(x) = f(0)$$

Case-III $\quad \alpha \notin \left[0, \frac{1}{2}\right]$

$$\beta \in \left[0, \frac{1}{2}\right]$$

In this case $\quad \alpha\beta < 0$

$$\Rightarrow \quad \Delta < 0 \Rightarrow \begin{cases} f^1(x) > 0, \forall x \in [0, \beta] \\ f^1(x) < 0 \, \forall x \in [\beta, \frac{1}{2}] \end{cases}$$

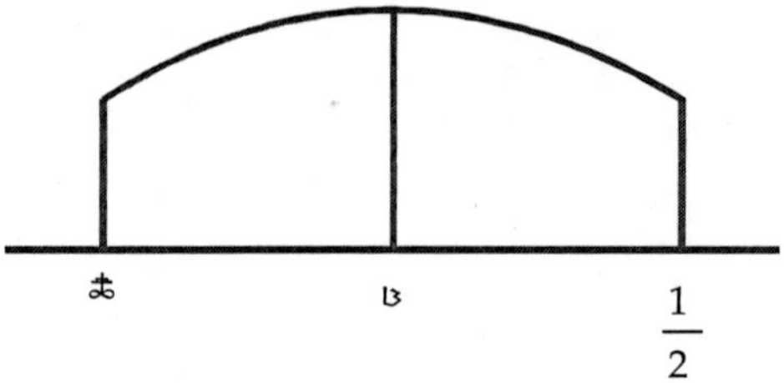

We have $\quad f(x) = f(\beta)$

$$x \in \{0, \beta]$$

max $\quad f(x) = f(\beta)$

$$x \in \left[\beta, \frac{1}{2}\right]$$

Hence max $\quad f(x) = f(\beta),$

$$\min f(x) = f(0)$$

Case-IV :

$$\alpha, \beta \in \left[0, \frac{1}{2}\right]$$

We show that this case is not possible. If possible let us assume that the roots are real and $0 < \alpha, \beta \leq \frac{1}{2}$

$$\Rightarrow \quad 0 < \alpha + \beta \leq 1$$

$$\Rightarrow \quad 0 < \frac{2w_3(w_2 - w_1)}{\Delta} \leq 1 \quad \text{...(9)}$$

Since $\quad \alpha\beta > 0$

We have $\quad \alpha\beta = \frac{w_2 w_3}{2\Delta} > 0$

$$\Rightarrow \quad \Delta > 0$$

$$\Rightarrow \quad w_2 > w_1 \text{ [by (9)]}$$

Also (9) $\Rightarrow$

$$2w_3 (w_2 - w_1) \leq \Delta$$

$$\Rightarrow \qquad w_3 \leq \frac{3\omega_1 w_2}{2w_1 + w_2} \qquad ...(10)$$

How the discriminant D of the equation (6) is :

$$D = w_3[(w_2^2 + 2w_1^2)w_3 - 3w_1w_2^2]$$

We have

$$(w_2^2 + 2w_1^2)w_3 - 3w_1w_2^2$$

$$\leq \frac{(w_2^2 + 2w_1)^2(3w_1w_2)}{2w_1 + w_2} - 3w_1w_2^2[\text{by}(10)]$$

$$\leq \frac{6w_1^2(w_1 - w_2)}{2w_1 + w_2} < 0$$

Hence, the roots are imaginary which contradicts the hypothesis of the case-IV. Hence case-IV is not possible.

$f(0), f\left(\frac{1}{2}\right), f(\alpha), f(\beta)$ can be expressed as follows :

$$f(0) = \frac{1}{6} \quad [\text{Putting } x = 0 \text{ and } \frac{1}{2} \text{ respectively in (2)}]$$

$$f\left(\frac{1}{2}\right) = \frac{w_1 + \frac{1}{3}w_3}{2(w_1 + w_3)},$$

α and β are given by

$$= \frac{2w_3(w_2 - w_1) \pm \sqrt{2w_2^2 w_3^2 + 4w_1^2w_3^2 - 6w_1w_2^2w_3}}{2(3w_1w_2 - 4w_1w_3 + w_2w_3)} \qquad ...(1)$$

where α is so choosen that $\alpha < \beta$.
Now $f(\alpha)$ or $f(\beta)$ can be evaluated by putting
$x =$ or $x =$ in (2) but it involves much calculations.
However $f(\alpha)$ or $f(\beta)$ can be obtained as follows :

$$\frac{ax^2 + bx + c}{a_1x^2 + b_1x + c_1} = y$$

$$(a - a_1y)x^2 + (b - b_1y)x + (c - c_1y) = 0$$

Since x is real the discriminant of this quadratic equation in x must be non-negative.

i.e. $(a - a_1y)\, x^2 + (b - b_1y)\, x + c - c_1y = 0$

i.e. $(b_1^2 - 4a_1c_1)y^2 + (4ac_1 + 4a_1c - 2bb_1)y + b^2 - 4ac \geq 0.$

The maximum and minimum values of y are roots of the equation.

$(b_1^2 - 4a_1c_1)y^2 + (4ac_1 + 4a_1c - 2bb_1)\,y + b^2 - 4ac = 0$

provided $b_1^2 - 4a_1c_1 \neq 0$

$$\text{i.e.} \quad y = \frac{-[2(ac_1 + a_1c) - bb_1) \pm 2\sqrt{(ac_1 - a_1c)^2 + (bc - b_1c)(a_1b - b_1a)}}{b_1^2 - 4a_1c_1}$$

substituting the values of $a, b\ c, a_1, b_1, c_1,$ from (1) we get

$$f(\alpha), f(\beta) = \frac{-\frac{4}{3}(2w_1w_3 + w_3^2 - 3w_2^2) \pm \sqrt{4w_1^2w_3^2 + w_3^2 - 6w_1w_2^2w_3}}{3(2w_2^2 - w_3^2 - w_1w_3)} \quad ...(12)$$

Provided $2w_2^2 - w_3^2 - w_1w_3 \neq 0$

where $f(\alpha)$ corresponds to positive or negative sign of the square root in (12) according as α corrsponds to the positive or negative signof the square root in the equation (11).

Finally we consider

Case-V $\Delta = 0$

$$\text{then} \quad f^1(x) = \frac{-2(ca_1 - c_1a)\,x + (bc_1 - b_1c)}{(a_1x^2 + b_1x + c_1)^2}$$

$$= \frac{w_3}{3\text{K}}[-4(w_2 - w_1)\,x + w_2]; \text{ where K} > 0$$

$$f^1(x) = 0, \text{ iff } x = \alpha = \frac{w_2}{4(w_2 - w_1)} \quad ...(13)$$

How we consider following cases :

$\text{V}_a\ \Delta = 0,\ w_2 < 2w_1$

If $\quad w_2\ £\ w_1$ then $\dfrac{w_2}{4(w_2 - w_1)} < 0$

Hence, $\alpha \notin \left[0, \frac{1}{2}\right]$.

In this case,

$$f^1(x) > 0, x \in \left[0, \frac{1}{2}\right].$$

If $w_2 > w_1$, then

$$\alpha = \frac{w_2}{4(w_2 - w_1)} = \frac{\frac{w_2}{w_1}}{4(\frac{w_2}{w_1} - 1} > 0$$

Also $$0 < \frac{w_2}{4(w_2 - w_1)} < \frac{1}{2}$$

$\Rightarrow$ $2w_2 < 4w_2 - 4w_1$

$\Rightarrow$ $2w_1 < w_2$

which is a contradiction.

Hence $$\alpha > \frac{1}{2} \Rightarrow \alpha \notin \left[0, \frac{1}{2}\right]$$

and again $f^1(x) > 0 \; \forall \, x \notin \left[0, \frac{1}{2}\right]$

Hence $\max f(x) = f\left(\frac{1}{2}\right)$,

$\min f(x) = f(0)$

V_b $\Delta = 0, w_2 > 2w_1$

In this case

$$0 < \alpha = \frac{w_2}{4(w_2 - w_1)} < \frac{1}{2}$$

Also $$f^1(x) \begin{cases} > 0, \text{if } x \in [0, \alpha] \\ < 0, \text{if } x \in [\alpha, \frac{1}{2}] \end{cases}$$

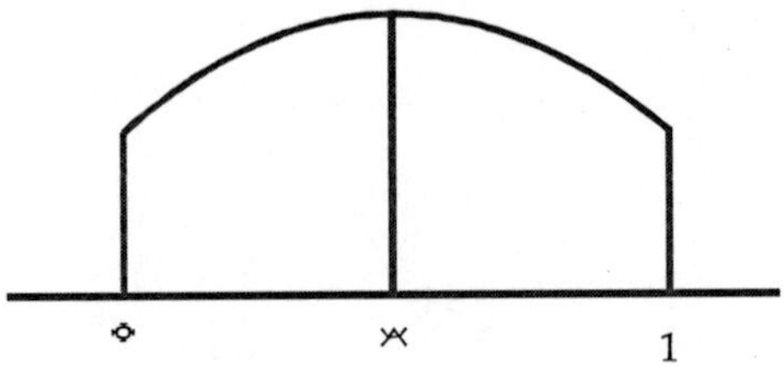

Hence $\max f(x) = f(\alpha)$

$\min f(x) = f(0)$

Consequences of the theorem I

(1) In the absence of selection,

$$\max f(x_1) = \frac{1}{3}, \min f(x_1) = \frac{1}{6}.$$

But in presence of selection, we note that by artificial selection $\max f(x_1)$ can be made to assume any value $\varepsilon]\frac{1}{6}, \frac{1}{2}[$ but, $\min f(x_1)$ remains the same i.e. $\frac{1}{6}$.

(2) If, $2w_2^2 \le w_3^2 + w_1 w_2$ then α, β are real.

Proof : $2_2^2 \le w_3^2 + w_1 w_3 \Leftrightarrow b_1^2 - 4a_1 c_1 < 0$

We know that α, β are the root of the equation

$(ab_1 - a_1 b)\, x^2 - 2\,(ca_1 - c_1 a)x + (bc_1 - b_1 c)$.

The discriminant of this equation is

$(a_1 c - ac_1)^2 - (ab_1 - a_1 b)\,(bc_1 - b_1 c)$

$$= c_1 a_1 [(\frac{c}{c_1} - \frac{a}{a_1})^2 (\frac{4c_1 a_1 - b_1^2}{4}) + \{b - \frac{b_1}{2}(\frac{c}{c_1} + \frac{a}{a_1})^2\}] \ge 0$$

Hence α, β are real.

(3) If $\quad 2w_2^2 = w_3^2 + w_1 w_3$

roots of the equation (6) are

$$\frac{w_2 w_3 (w_2 + w_3)}{(w_2 + w_3)^2 (6w_2 + 4w_3)}, \frac{w_3}{2(w_3 - w_2)}$$

Minimum and maximum values of $x_1^{(1)}$ in different cases are presented in the following table.

SI No.	Value of w_1, w_2, w_3	α	β	Case No.	Va lye X	Value of $x_1(1)$	minimum	Maximum
1.	$w_1 = \frac{1}{3}$	$\frac{-2-\sqrt{-5880998}}{58798}$	I_a		0	$\frac{1}{2}$	$\frac{1}{6}$	$\frac{301}{606}$
	$w_2 = \frac{90}{100}$	$\frac{-2+\sqrt{-5880998}}{58798}$						
	$w_3 = \frac{1}{100}$							
2.	$w_1 = 1/4$	$\frac{2-\sqrt{146}}{17}$	$\frac{2+\sqrt{146}}{17}$	I_b	0	$\frac{1}{2}$	$\frac{1}{6}$	$\frac{1}{4}$
	$w_2 = 1/6$							
	$w_3 = 1$							
3.	$w_1 = 7/15$	$\frac{-13+\sqrt{109}}{8}$	$\frac{-13-\sqrt{109}}{8}$	I_c	0	$\frac{1}{2}$	$\frac{1}{6}$	$\frac{2}{5}$
	$w_2 = 1/4$							
	$w_3 = 1/5$							
4.	$w_1 = 1$	$-\frac{1}{2}$	$-\frac{1}{2}$	I_d	0	$\frac{1}{2}$	$\frac{1}{6}$	$\frac{5}{12}$
	$w_2 = 1/2$							
	$W_3 = 1/3$							
5.	$w_1 = 1/10$	$\frac{5}{14}$	$\frac{5}{2}$	II	0	$\frac{5}{14}$	$\frac{1}{6}$	$\frac{13}{60}$
	$w_2 = 1/2$							
	$w_3 = 5/6$							
6.	$w_1 = 1/3$	$-\frac{3}{2}$	$\frac{1}{2}$	III	0	$\frac{1}{2}$	$\frac{1}{6}$	$\frac{1}{4}$
	$w_2 = 1/2$							
	$w_3 = 1$	$\frac{7}{20}$		V_a	0	$\frac{1}{2}$	$\frac{1}{6}$	$\frac{2}{11}$
7.	$w_1 = 1/21$							
	$w_2 = 1/6$							
	$w_3 = 1$							
8.	$w_1 = 1/5$	$\frac{5}{12}$		V_b	0	$\frac{5}{12}$	$\frac{1}{6}$	$\frac{5}{7}$
	$w_2 = 1/2$							
	$w_3 = 1$							

Table-6

Therom II : Under the conditions (I), (II) and (III) the maximum value of x_1(the frequency of $a_1 a_1$) in the generation is :

$\mu_1^{(n)}$ given inductively by

$\mu_1^{(1)} = \max\ x_1^{(1)}$

= the value of x_1 in the first generation given by theorem I.

$\mu_1^{(r)} = f(\mu_1^{(x-1)}$ where r =2, 3,.......n.

Proof : In the transition from initial generation to first generation the range of the evolution function f is $[f(0), f\left(\frac{1}{2}\right)]$ in case I of theorem I and is $[(0), f(\alpha)]$in case IIof theorem I. Both the intervals are compact on which the function f is Monotonically increasing. Hence in the next generation the maximum and minimum value of f will be attained at upper and lower ends of the interval respectively. Hence in the second generation the minimum and maximum values of f $(f(x_1)] = f^2(x_1)$ is f^2 (0) and $f^2\left(\frac{1}{2}\right)$ in caseI and f^2 (0) and f^2 (α) in case-II. After the Ist generation we note that in transitions from each generation to filial generation f is Monotonically increasing in the corresponding compact domain.Hence in case I of theorem I the minimum values of the frequency of a_1a_1 are f (0), 02(0), in different generations. On the other hand case-II of theorem I and maximum values of the same are $f(\alpha)$, f^2 (α)........., in different generations.

Hence the theorem.

Theorem-III : Under the condition (I), (II) and (III) the maximum and minimum the values of the frequency of a_1a_1 tend to the same equilibrium value.

Proof : It is clear that the equilibrium value of x_1 (the frequency of a_1a_1) corresponds to an idompotent in the algebraa representing the inheritance of tetraploidy.

By equation(2) of the theorem I the equilibrium value of x_1 is a root of the equation :

$$x = \frac{Ax^2 + Bx + c}{A_1x^2 + B_1x + C_1} \quad ...(1)$$

where $\quad 0 \le x \le \frac{1}{2}$

and the maximum value of the same as $f\left(\frac{1}{2}\right)$ $f^2\left(\frac{1}{2}\right)$

$$A = w_1 - 2w_2 + w_3$$

$$B = w_2 - \frac{2}{3}w_3$$

$$C = \frac{1}{6}w_3$$

$$A_1 = 2w_1 - 3w_2 + 6w_3$$
$$B_1 = 4(w_2 - w_3)$$
$$C_1 = w_3$$

It is clear that the equilibrium of x_1 is unique if and only if the equation (I) has one and only one root i.e. it is sufficient to prove the following lemma.

Lemma : The equation

$$f(x) = a_0x^3 - 3a_1x^2 + 3a_2x - a_3 = 0 \qquad ...(1)$$

where

$$a_0 = 2w_1 - 8w_2 + 6w_3$$

$$a_1 = \frac{w_1 - 6w_2 + 5w_3}{3}$$

$$a_2 = \frac{5}{9}w_3 - \frac{w_2}{3} \qquad ...(2)$$

$$a_3 = \frac{1}{6}w_3$$

$0 < w_1, w_2, w_3$ £ 1

has one and only one root lying between 0 and $\frac{1}{2}$.

Proof of the Lemma :

We have $f(0) = -\frac{1}{6}w_3 < 0$

$$f\left(\frac{1}{2}\right) = \frac{1}{3}a_0 - \frac{3}{4}a_1 + \frac{3}{2}a_2 - a_3$$

$$= \frac{1}{3}(2w_1 - 8w_2 + 6w_3) - \frac{1}{4}(w_1 - 6w_2 + 5w_3) + \frac{3}{2}\left(\frac{5}{9}w_3 - \frac{w_2}{3}\right) - \frac{1}{6}w_3$$

$$= \frac{1}{6}w_3 > 0$$

From real analysis, it is clear that the equation $f(x) = 0$ has either one real root or three real roots between 0 and 1/2. If possible let there be three real roots α, β, γ between 0 and1/2.

We have

$$\alpha + \beta + \gamma = \frac{3a_1}{a_0}$$

$$\alpha\beta + \beta\gamma + \gamma\alpha = \frac{3a_2}{a_0}$$

$$\alpha\beta\gamma = \frac{a_3}{a_0}$$

$$\beta + \gamma = \frac{3a_1}{a_0} - \alpha \le 1$$

$$\beta\gamma = \frac{1}{\alpha}\frac{a_3}{a_0} \le \frac{1}{4} \qquad \text{...(3)}$$

Hence β, γ are real,

$$\left(\frac{3a_1}{a_0} - \alpha\right)^2 - \frac{4}{\alpha}\left(\frac{a_3}{a_e}\right) \ge 0 \qquad \text{...(4)}$$

$$0 < \frac{3a_1}{a_0} - \alpha \le 1$$

i.e. $$\frac{3a_1}{a_0} = 1 + \alpha - k \ ; \ 0 \pounds k < 1 \qquad \text{...(5)}$$

$$\frac{1}{\alpha}.\frac{a_3}{a_0} \le \frac{1}{4}$$

$$\frac{a_3}{a_0} \le \frac{\alpha}{4}$$

$$\frac{a_3}{a_0} = \frac{0\alpha}{4}, 0 < \theta \le 1 \qquad \text{...(6)}$$

$$\frac{\theta\alpha}{4} = \frac{a_3}{a_0}$$

$$\alpha(1-k)+\frac{\theta}{4} = \frac{3a_2}{a_0}$$

$$1+\alpha-k = \frac{3a_1}{a_0}$$

Now from (4) we have

$$(1-k)^2 - \frac{4}{\alpha}\left(\frac{\theta\alpha}{4}\right) \geq 0$$

$$(1-k)^2 - \theta \geq 0 \qquad \text{...(7)}$$

Now from (2), we have

$$\frac{\theta\alpha}{4} = \frac{\frac{1}{6}w_3}{2w_1 - 8w_2 + 6w_3}$$

$$\alpha(1-k)+\frac{\theta}{4} = \frac{\frac{5}{3}w_3 - w_2}{2w_1 - 8w_2 + 6w_3}$$

$$1+\alpha-k = \frac{w_1 - 6w_2 + 5w_3}{2w_1 - 8w_2 + 6w_3}$$

i.e.

$$\frac{5}{2}\theta\alpha = \frac{5}{3}\cdot\frac{w_3}{a_0}$$

$$\alpha(1-k)+\frac{\theta}{4} = \frac{\frac{5}{3}w_3 - w_2}{a_0}$$

From these we obtain

$$\frac{w_1}{a_0} = 1+\alpha-k+15\theta\alpha-6\alpha(1-k)-\frac{3}{2}\theta-\frac{15}{2}\theta\alpha \qquad \text{...(8)}$$

$$\frac{w_2}{a_0} = \frac{5}{2}\theta\alpha-\alpha(1-k)-\frac{\theta}{4} \qquad \text{...(9)}$$

$$\frac{w_3}{a_0} = \frac{3}{2}\theta\alpha \qquad \text{...(10)}$$

Multiplying equation (8) by 2, equation (9) by − 8 and equation (10) by 6 and adding all there we get

$$\theta = \frac{(1-2\alpha)(2k-1)}{(4\alpha-1)} \qquad \text{...(11)}$$

Putting $\quad \theta = \dfrac{(1-2\alpha)}{(4\alpha-1)}(2k-1)$

in equation (9) we get

$$\frac{w_2}{a_0} = \frac{5}{2}\theta\alpha - \alpha(1-k) - \frac{\theta}{4}$$

$$= \frac{5}{2}\frac{(1-2\alpha)(2k-1)\alpha}{(4\alpha-1)} - \alpha(1-k) - \frac{(1-2\alpha)(2k-1)}{4(4\alpha-1)}$$

i.e. $\dfrac{4w_2(4\alpha-1)}{a_0} = (-24\alpha^2+20\alpha-2)k + 4\alpha^2 - 8\alpha + 1 \qquad \text{...(12)}$

How we consider the following cases

Case-I : $\dfrac{1}{4} < \alpha < \dfrac{1}{2}$

From (12), we have

$(-24\alpha^2+20\alpha-2)\,k > -4\alpha^2+8\alpha-1$

$$\therefore \quad k > \frac{-4\alpha^2+8\alpha-1}{2(-12\alpha^2+10\alpha-1)} \qquad \text{...(13)}$$

From (7) and (11) we have

$$(1-k)^2 - \theta \geq 0$$

$$(1-k)^2 \geq \frac{(1-2\alpha)(2k-1)}{4\alpha-1}$$

$$(4\alpha-1)k^2 - 4\alpha k + 2\alpha \geq 0 \qquad \text{...(14)}$$

The roots of the corresponding quadratic equation are

$$= \frac{4\alpha \pm \sqrt{16\alpha^2 - 4(4\alpha-1)2\alpha}}{2(4\alpha-1)}$$

$$= \frac{2\alpha \pm \sqrt{-4\alpha^2+2\alpha}}{(4\alpha-1)}$$

Since the discriminant of (14) is positive,

$$k \geq \frac{2\alpha + \sqrt{2\alpha - 4\alpha^2}}{(4\alpha - 1)} \qquad \text{(not admissible)}$$

or

$$k \leq \frac{2\alpha - \sqrt{2\alpha - 4\alpha^2}}{(4\alpha - 1)}$$

Hence from (13) we have

$$\frac{2\alpha - \sqrt{2\alpha(1-2\alpha)}}{(4\alpha - 1)} > \frac{-4\alpha^2 + 8\alpha - 1}{2(-12\alpha^2 + 10\alpha - 1)}$$

i.e.

$$\frac{4\alpha}{2\alpha + \sqrt{2\alpha(1-2\alpha)}} > \frac{-4\alpha^2 + 8\alpha - 1}{-12\alpha^2 + 10\alpha - 1}$$

i.e.

$$\frac{2\alpha + \sqrt{2\alpha(1-2\alpha)}}{4\alpha} < \frac{-12\alpha^2 + 10\alpha - 1}{-4\alpha^2 + 8\alpha - 1}$$

Putting $\alpha = \left(\beta + \frac{1}{4}\right)$ we have

$$\frac{1}{2}\sqrt{\frac{1-4\beta}{1+4\beta}} + \frac{1}{2} < \frac{12\left(\beta + \frac{1}{4}\right)^2 - 10\left(\beta + \frac{1}{4}\right) + 1}{4\left(\beta + \frac{1}{4}\right)^2 - 8\left(\beta + \frac{1}{4}\right) + 1} \quad \text{where } 0 < \beta < \frac{1}{4}$$

Now putting $\gamma = \sqrt{\frac{1-4\beta}{1+4\beta}}$

i.e. $4\beta = \frac{1-\gamma}{1+\gamma}$ we have

$$\sqrt{\gamma} < \frac{-\gamma^2 + 4\gamma}{-\gamma^2 + 2\gamma + 2}, \text{ where } 0 < \gamma < 1$$

Let $\sqrt{\gamma} = \delta, \gamma = \alpha^2$

$$\delta < \frac{-8^4 + 4\delta^2}{-\delta^4 + 2\delta^2 + 2}, 0 < \delta < 1$$

$-x^4 + x^3 + 2x^2 - 4x + 2 < 0$

(since $x^{-4} + 2x^2 + 2 > 0$, where $0 < x < 1$]

$x^3(1 - x) - 2x(1 - x) + 2(1 - x) < 0$

$x^3 - 2x + 2 < 0$ ...(15)

But $x^2 - 2x + 2 > x^3 - 2 + 2 = x^3 > 0$

Hence, (15) is a contradiction.

Case-II : $\alpha < \frac{1}{4}$ [i.e. $k < \frac{1}{2}$ by (10)]

Since $-24\alpha^2 + 20\alpha - 2 \leq 0$ according as $\frac{5-\sqrt{13}}{12} \geq \alpha$ following subcases arise

Case-II$_a$: $\frac{2-\sqrt{3}}{2} < \alpha < \frac{1}{4}$

From (12) we have $\alpha > \frac{2-\sqrt{3}}{2}$

and $k < \frac{-4\alpha^2 + 8\alpha - 1}{2(-12\alpha^2 + 10\alpha - 1)}$ ...(13)[1]

From (7), we get

$$(1-k)^2 \geq \frac{(1-2\alpha)(1-2k)}{(1-4\alpha)}$$

$(1-4\alpha)(1-k)^2 \geq (1-2\alpha)(1-2k)$

i.e. $(1-4\alpha)k^2 + 4\alpha k - 2\alpha \geq 0$ ....(14)[1]

The roots of the corresponding quadratic equations are

$$\frac{-2\alpha \pm \sqrt{2\alpha(1-2\alpha)}}{(1-4\alpha)}$$

Since the discriminant of (14)[1] is positive or zero, we must have

$k \leq \frac{-2\alpha - \sqrt{2\alpha(1-2\alpha)}}{1-4\alpha} < 0$ (not admissible)

or $$k \geq \frac{-2\alpha + \sqrt{2\alpha(1-2\alpha)}}{(1-4\alpha)}$$

Hence from (13)[1] we have

$$\frac{-2\alpha+\sqrt{2\alpha(1-2\alpha)}}{1-4\alpha}<\frac{-4\alpha^2+8\alpha-1}{2(-12\alpha^2+10\alpha-1)}$$

$$\frac{4\alpha}{\sqrt{2\alpha(1-2\alpha)}+2\alpha}<\frac{-4\alpha^2+8\alpha-1}{-12\alpha^2+10\alpha-1}$$

$$\frac{2\alpha+\sqrt{2\alpha(1-2\alpha)}}{4\alpha}<\frac{-12\alpha^2+10\alpha-1}{-4\alpha^2+8\alpha-1}$$

Putting $\alpha=\frac{1}{4}-\beta$, where $0<\beta<\frac{-2+\sqrt{13}}{13}$

$$\frac{1}{2}\sqrt{\frac{1+4\beta}{1-4\beta}}+\frac{1}{2}>\frac{12\left(\frac{1}{4}\beta\right)^2-10\left(\frac{1}{4}-\beta\right)+1}{4\left(\frac{1}{4}-\beta\right)^2-8\left(\frac{1}{4}-\beta\right)+1}$$

Again putting

$$\gamma=\frac{1+4\beta}{1-4\beta}$$

$\sqrt{\gamma}>\frac{4\gamma-\gamma^2}{2+2\gamma-\gamma^2}$, where $1+\gamma<\frac{2+\sqrt{13}}{2}=2,8027$

Let $\sqrt{\gamma}=\delta, 1<\delta<1,6741492$

$$\delta>\frac{4\delta^2-\delta^4}{2+2\delta^2-\delta^4}$$

□ $\alpha>2-\frac{\sqrt{3}}{2}$

□ $\gamma<1+\sqrt{3}$ [By the relation $\varkappa=\frac{1}{2(\gamma+1)}$]

□ $2+2\gamma-\gamma^2>0$

□ $2+2\delta^2-\delta^4>0$

$2\delta+2\delta^3-\delta^5>4\delta^2-\delta^4$

□ $\delta^5-\delta^4-2\delta^3+4\delta^2-2\delta<0$

□ $(\delta-1)(\delta^3-2\delta+2)<0$

□ $\delta^3-2\delta+2<0$ ...(15)1

$f(\delta)=\delta^3-2\delta+2>0$, if $=1$

Also $f^1(\delta)=3\delta^2-2>0$ for $1<\delta<\sqrt{\frac{2+\sqrt{13}}{2}}$

Hence if $(\delta)>0$, for $\Delta<\delta=\sqrt{\frac{2+\sqrt{13}}{2}}$ and so $(15)^1$ is a contradiction.

Case II$_b$: $\frac{5-\sqrt{13}}{2}\le\alpha\le\frac{2-\sqrt{3}}{2}$

$-4\alpha^2+8\alpha-1\ge 0$ if $\frac{2-\sqrt{3}}{2}\le\alpha\le\frac{2+\sqrt{3}}{2}$

$-12\alpha^2+10\alpha-1\ge 0$ if $\frac{5-\sqrt{13}}{12}\le\alpha\le\frac{5+\sqrt{13}}{12}$

$\frac{5-\sqrt{13}}{2}=.11,6204$

$\frac{2-\sqrt{3}}{2}=.1339746>\frac{5-\sqrt{13}}{2}$

In this case $-4\alpha^2+8\alpha-1\le 0$

$-12\alpha^2+10a-1\ge 0$

From (12), it is clear that this case in not possible.

Case II$_c$: $\alpha<\frac{5-\sqrt{13}}{2}=.116204$

In this case

$(-24\alpha^2+20\alpha-2)\,k+4\alpha^2-8\alpha+1<0$

□ $(24\alpha^2-20\alpha+2)\,k-4\alpha^2+8\alpha-1>0$

□ $k>\frac{4\alpha^2-8\alpha+1}{24\alpha^2-20\alpha+2}$ ...(13)

□ $$\frac{4\alpha^2-8\alpha+1}{2(12\alpha^2-10\alpha+1)}<\frac{1}{2}$$

□ $4\alpha^2-8\alpha+1<12\alpha^2-10\alpha+1$

□ $8\alpha^2-2\alpha>0$

i.e. $2\alpha(4\alpha-1)>0$

i.e. $$\alpha>\frac{1}{4}$$

which is a contradiction

Hence $$\frac{4\alpha^2-8\alpha+1}{24\alpha^2-20\alpha+2}>\frac{1}{2}$$

□ $$k>\frac{1}{2}[\text{by }(13)^{11}]$$

□ $\theta<0[\text{by }(11)]$

which contradicts (6)

As explained earlier the theorem III follows at once from the Lemma.

Chapter-5

GAMETIC ALGEBRA OF HEXA-PLOIDY UNDER SELECTION

5.1 Inheritance of Hexa-Ploidy with Selection

In this chapter we consider in infinite random mating population of hexaploid individuals which differ in a single locus with two alleles a_1, a_2. The 3-ploid gametes produced by the population are $a_1a_1a_1$, $a_1a_1a_2 + a_1a_2a_2$ and $a_2a_2a_2$ which will abbreviated as a_{11}, of the gametes is given by the following table :

	a_{11}	${}_1a_{112}$	a_{122}	a_{222}
a_{111}	a_{111}	$\frac{1}{2}(a_{111}+a_{112})$	$\frac{1}{5}a_{111}+\frac{3}{5}a_{112}$ $+\frac{1}{5}a_{122}$	$\frac{1}{20}a_{111}+\frac{9}{20}a_{112}$ $+\frac{9}{20}a+\frac{1}{20}a_{222}$
a_{112}		$\frac{1}{5}a_{111}+\frac{3}{5}a_{112}+\frac{1}{5}a_{122}$	$\frac{1}{20}a_{111}+\frac{9}{20}a_{112}$ $+\frac{9}{20}a_{122}+\frac{1}{20}a_{222}$	$\frac{1}{5}a_{112}+\frac{3}{5}a_{122}$ $+\frac{1}{5}a_{222}$
a_{122}			$\frac{1}{5}a_{112}+\frac{3}{5}a_{122}$ $+\frac{1}{5}a_{222}$	$\frac{1}{2}(a_{122}+a_{222})$
a_{222}				a_{222}

Table-1

In presence of selection the segregation behaviour of the gametes is given by the following table $(0 £ w_{ij} £ i)$

	a_{111}	a_{112}	$a_{112}a_{122}$	a_{222}
a_{111}	$w_{11}\ a_{111}$	$\frac{1}{2}w_{12}(a_{111}+a_{112})$	$w_{13}(\frac{1}{5}a_{111}+\frac{3}{5}a_{112}$ $+\frac{1}{5}a_{122})$	$w_{14}(\frac{1}{20}a_{111}+$ $\frac{9}{20}a_{112}+\frac{9}{20}a_{122}$ $+\frac{1}{20}a_{222})$
a_{112}	$\frac{1}{2}w_{21}$ $(a_{111}+a_{112})$	$w_{22}(\frac{1}{5}a_{111}+\frac{3}{5}a_{112}$ $+\frac{1}{5}a_{122}\ +\frac{1}{5}a_{122})$	$w_{23}(\frac{1}{20}a_{111}+$ $\frac{9}{20}a_{122}+\frac{9}{20}a_{22}$ $+\frac{1}{20}a_{222})$	$w_{24}(\frac{1}{5}a_{111}$ $+\frac{3}{5}a_{112}+\frac{3}{5}a_{122}$ $+\frac{1}{5}a_{222})$
a_{122}	$w_{31}(\frac{1}{5}a_{111}$ $+\frac{3}{5}a_{112}$ $+\frac{1}{5}a_{122})$	$w_{32}(\frac{1}{20}a_{111}$ $+\frac{9}{20}a_{112}+\frac{9}{20}a_{122}$ $+\frac{1}{20}a_{222)}$	$w_{33}(\frac{1}{5}a_{112}+\frac{3}{5}a_{122}$ $+\frac{1}{5}a_{222})$	$\frac{1}{2}w_{34}\ (a_{122}+a_{222})$
a_{222}	$w_{41}(\frac{1}{20}a_{111}$ $+\frac{9}{20}a_{112}$ $+\frac{9}{20}a_{112}$ $+\frac{1}{20}a_{222})$	$w_{42}(\frac{1}{5}a_{112}\ +\frac{3}{5}a_{122}$ $+\frac{1}{5}a_{222})$	$\frac{1}{2}w_{43}(a_{122}+a_{222})$	$w_{44}a_{222}$

Remarks : 1. If the segregation behaviour is symetric i.e.

ahij $a_{k1m} = a_{k1m} a_{hij}$

then we assume $w_{ij} = w_{ji}$

2. If we assume that

(*i*) Zygotes (union of two gametes) containing same alleleles have same segregation behaviour.

(*ii*) If the alleless are interchanged, than the segregation behaviour of a zygote remains unchanged then

$$w_{11} = w_{44} = w_1$$
$$w_{12} = w_{21} = w_{34} = w_{43} = w_2$$
$$w_{31} = w_{13} = w_{22} = w_{24} = w_{42} = w_{33} = w_3$$
$$w_{14} = w_{41} = w_{23} = w_{32} = w_4$$

5.2 The Evoluation Equation :

We assume that $w_{ij} = w_{ji}$

Let $x = x_1 a_{111} + x_2 a_{112} + x_3 a_{122} + x_4 a_{222}$ represent the state of a population in the initial generation.

The state of the population in the next generation is given by

$$x^2 = (x_1 a_{111} + x_2 a_{112} + x_3 a_{122} + x_4 a_{222})^2$$

$$= x_1^2 a_{111}^2 + x_2^2 a_{112}^2 + x_3^2 a_{122}^2 + x_4^2 a_{222}^2$$
$$+ 2x_1 x_2 a_{111} a_{112} + 2x_3 3x_4 a_{122} a_{222} + 2x_1 x_3 a_{111} a_{122}$$
$$+ 2x_1 x_4 a_{111} a_{222} + 2x_2 x_3\, 3a_{112} a_{122} + 2x_1 x_4\, a_{112}\, a_{222}$$

$$= x_1^2 w_{11} a_{111} + x_2^2 w_{22} (\frac{1}{5} a_{111} + \frac{3}{5} a_{112} + \frac{1}{5} a_{122})$$

$$+ x_3^2 w_{33} (\frac{1}{5} a_{112} + \frac{3}{5} a_{122} + \frac{1}{5} a_{222}) + x_4^2\, w_{44} a_{222}$$

$$+ x_1 x_2 w_{12} (a_{111} + a_{112}) + x_3 x_4 w_{34} (a_{122} + a_{222})$$

$$+ 2x_1 x_3 w_{13} (\frac{1}{5} a_{111} + \frac{3}{5} a_{112} + \frac{1}{5} a_{122})$$

$$+ 2x_1 x_4 w_{14} (\frac{1}{20} a_{111} + \frac{9}{20} a_{112} + \frac{9}{20} a_{122} + \frac{1}{20} a_{222})$$

$$+ 2x_2 x_3 w_{23} (\frac{1}{20} a_{111} + \frac{9}{20} a_{112} + \frac{9}{20} a_{122} + \frac{1}{20} a_{222})$$

$$+ 2x_2 x_4\, w_{23} (\frac{1}{5} a_{112} + \frac{3}{5} a_{122} + \frac{1}{5} a_{222})$$

$$x^2 = (x_1^2 w_{11} + \frac{1}{5}x_2^2 w_{22} + x_1 x_2 w_{12} + \frac{2}{5}x_1 x_3 w_{13}$$

$$+\frac{1}{10}x_1 x_4 w_{14} + \frac{1}{10}x_2 x_3 w_{23})a_{111} + (\frac{3}{5}x_2^2 w_{22} + \frac{1}{5}x_3^2 w_{33}$$

$$+ x_1 x_2 w_{12} + \frac{6}{5}x_1 x_3 w_{13} + \frac{9}{10}x_1 x_4 w_{14} + \frac{9}{10}x_2 x_3 w_{23}$$

$$+\frac{2}{5}x_2 x_4 w_{24})a_{112}$$

$$+ (\frac{1}{5}x_2^2 w_{22} + \frac{3}{5}x_3^2 w_{33} + x_3 x_4 w_{34} + \frac{2}{5}x_1 x_3 w_{13}$$

$$+ \frac{9}{10}x_1 x_4 w_{14} + \frac{9}{10}x_2 x_3 w_{23} + \frac{10}{5}x_2 x_4 w_{24})a_{122}$$

$$+ (\frac{1}{5}x_3^2 w_{33} + x_4^2 w_{44} + x_3 x_4 w_{34} + \frac{1}{10}x_1 x_4 w_{14}$$

$$+ \frac{1}{10}x_2 x_3 w_{23} + \frac{2}{5}x_2 x_4 w_{24})a_{222} \quad \text{...(1)}$$

If $x_1 + x_2 + x_3 + x_4 = 1$, then the equation in normalized form is

$$x^2 = \frac{1}{w}[x_1^2 w_{11} + \frac{1}{5}x_2^2 w_{22} + x_1 x_2 w_{12} + \frac{2}{5}x_1 x_3 w_{13}$$

$$+\frac{1}{10}x_1 x_4 w_{14} + \frac{1}{10}x_2 x_3 w_{33})a_{111} + (\frac{3}{5}x_2^2 w_{22} + \frac{1}{5}x_3^2 w_{33}$$

$$+ x_1 x_2 w_{12} + \frac{6}{5}x_1 x_3 w_{13} + \frac{9}{10}x_1 x_4 w_{14} + \frac{9}{10}x_2 x_3 w_{22}$$

$$+ \frac{2}{5}x_3 x_4 w_{24})a_{112} + (\frac{1}{5}x_2^2 w_{22} + \frac{3}{5}x_3^2 w_{33} + x_3 x_4 w_{34}$$

$$+ \frac{2}{5}x_1 x_3 w_{13} + \frac{9}{10}x_1 x_4 w_{14} + \frac{9}{10}x_2 x_3 w_{23} + \frac{6}{3}x_2 x_4 w_{24})a_{122}$$

$$+ (\frac{1}{5}x_3^2 w_{33} + x_4^2 w_{44} + x_3 x_4 w_{34} + \frac{1}{10}x_1 x_4 w_{14}$$

$$+\frac{1}{10}x_2x_3w_{23}+\frac{2}{5}x_2w_{24})a_{222} \qquad ...(8)$$

Where $w = x_1^2w_{11}+x_2^2w_{22}+x_3^2w_{33}+x_4^2w_{44}+2x_1x_2w_{12}$

$$+2x_2x_3w_{23}+2x_1x_3w_{31}+2x_1x_4w_{14}+2x_4x_4w_{24}$$

$$+\ 2x_3x_4w_{34}$$

5.3 Simplification of the Evolution Equation

In absence of selection (*i.e.* $w_{ij} = 1$) it is known that the evolution equation is much simplified if we change the basis $(a_{111}, a_{112}, a_{122}, a_{222})$ □ (c_0, c_1, c_2, c_3) by the self inverse transformation

$$\begin{aligned} c_0 &= a_{111} \\ c_1 &= a_{111} - a_{112} \\ c_2 &= a_{111} - 2a_{112} + a_{122} \\ c_3 &= a_{111} - 3a_{112} + 3a_{122} - a_{222} \end{aligned} \qquad ...(3)$$

Hence we obtain the equation reduced by the transformation (3) in some special cases.

Case-I, $\quad W_{11} = 1 - s_1$

$W_{44} = 1 - s_2$

$W_{ij} = 1$, if i, j □ $11, 44$

We assume that $x_1 + x_2 + x_3 + x_4 = 1$ than the equation (2) is

$$x^2 = \frac{1}{w}[\{1-s_1)x_1^2+\frac{1}{5}x_2^2+x_1x_2+\frac{2}{5}x_1x_3+\frac{1}{10}x_1x_4$$

$$+\frac{1}{10}x_2x_3\}a_{111}+(\frac{3}{5}x_2^2+\frac{1}{5}x_3^2+x_1x_2+\frac{6}{5}x_1x_3$$

$$+\frac{9}{10}x_1x_4+\frac{9}{10}x_2x_3+\frac{2}{5}x_2x_4)a_{112}+(\frac{1}{5}x_2^2+\frac{3}{5}x_3^2$$

$$+x_2x_4+\frac{2}{5}x_1x_3+\frac{9}{10}x_1x_4+\frac{9}{10}x_2x_3+\frac{6}{5}x_2x_4)a_{132}$$

$$+\ \{(\frac{1}{5}-x_3^2w_{33}+x_3x_4w_{34}+\frac{1}{10}x_1x_4+\frac{1}{10}x_2x_3+x_4^2(1-s_2)\}a_{222}]$$

Where $w = (x_1 + x_2 + x_3 + x_4)^2 - s_1 x_1^2 - s_2 x_4^2$

$= 1 - s_1 x_1^2 - s_2 x_4^2$

The equation in the normalize form is

$$\frac{x^2}{\| x \|} = \frac{1}{w}(c_0 - y_1 c_1 + y_2 c_2 + y_3 c_3)^2$$

Where $y_1 = x_2 + 2x_3 + 3x_4$

$y_2 = x_3 + 3x_4$

$y_3 = x_4$

From the table 2, we construct the following table for the composition of c_0, c_1, c_2, c_3.

	c_0	c_1	c_2	c_3
c_0	$(1-s_1)c_0$	$-(s_1c_0 - \frac{1}{2}c_1)$	$-s_1c_0 + \frac{1}{5}c_2$	$-s_1c_0 + \frac{1}{20}c_2$
c_1		$-s_1c_0 + \frac{1}{5}c_2$	$-s_1c_0 + \frac{1}{20}c_3$	$-s_1c_0$
c_2			$-s_1c_0$	$-s_1c_0$
c_3				$-s_1c_0 - s_2(c_0 - 3c_1 + 3c_2 - c_1)$

Table-3

$$\frac{x^2}{\| x^2 \|} = \frac{1}{w}(c_0 - y_1c_1 + y_2c_2 - y_3c_3)^2$$

$$= \frac{1}{w}[(c_0 - y_1c_1)^2 + 2(c_0 - y_1c_1)(y_2c_2 - y_3c_3) + (y_2c_2 - y_3c_3)^2]$$

$$= c_0^2 - 2y_1c_0c_1 + y_1^2c_1^2 + 2y_2c_0c_2 - 2c_0c_3y_3 - 2y_1y_2c_1c_2$$

$$+ 2y_1y_3c_1c_3 - 2y_1y_2c_1c_2 + 2y_1y_3c_1c_3 + y_2^2c_2^2 - 2y_2y_3c_2c_3 + y_3^2c_3^2$$

$$= (1-s_1)c_0 - 2y_1(-s_1c_0 + \frac{1}{2}c_1) + y_1^2(-s_1c_0 + \frac{1}{5}c_2)$$

$$+ 2y_2(-s_1c_0 + \frac{1}{5}c_2) - 2y_3(-s_1c_0 + \frac{1}{20}c_3)$$

$$-2y_1y_2(-s_1c_0+\frac{1}{20}c_3)+2y_1y_3(-s_1c_0)+y_2^2(-s_1c_0)$$

$$-2y_2y_3(-s_1c_0)+y_3^2(-s_1c_0)-s_2(c_0-3c_1+3c_2-c_3)$$

$$=(1+2y_1s_1-y_1^2s_1-2y_2s_1+2y_3s_1+2y_1y_2s_1-2y_1y_3s_1$$

$$-y_2^2s_1+2y_2y_3s_1-y_3^2s_1-s_2y_3^2)c_0-(y_1-3s_2y_3^2)c_1$$

$$+(\frac{1}{5}y_1^2+\frac{2}{5}y_2-3s_2y_3^2)c_2-(\frac{1}{10}y_3+\frac{1}{10}y_1y_2-y_3^2s_2)c_3$$

$$=c_0-\frac{1}{w}(y_1-3y_3^2s_2)c_1+\frac{1}{w}(\frac{1}{5}y_1^2+\frac{2}{5}y_2-3s_2y_3^2)c_2$$

$$-\frac{1}{w}(\frac{1}{10}y_3+\frac{1}{10}y_1y_2-y_3^2s_2)c_3$$

where $w=1-s_1(1+y_1-y_2+y_3)^2-s_2y_3^2$

Hence the reduced normalized equation in coordinate form is

$$y_1^1=\frac{1}{w}(y_1-3y_3^2s_2)$$

$$y_2^1=\frac{1}{w}(\frac{1}{5}y_1^2+\frac{2}{5}y_2-3s_2y_3^2)$$

$$y_3^1=\frac{1}{w}(\frac{1}{10}y_3+\frac{1}{10}y_1y_2-y_3^2s_2) \quad \text{...(4)}$$

Case-II : Zyogtes containing same alleles have same segregation behaviour and if the alleles are interchanged the segregation behaviour of a zygote remains unchanged.

i.e., $w_{11}=w_{44}=w_1$

$w_{12}=w_{21}=w_{34}=w_{43}=w_2$

$w_{31}=w_{13}=w_{24}=w_{42}=w_{22}=w_{33}=w_3$

$w_{14}=w_{41}=w_{23}=w_{32}=w_4$

The multiplication table is

	a_{111}	a_{112}	a_{122}	a_{222}
a_{111}	$w_1 a_{111}$	$\frac{1}{2}w_2(a_{111}+a_{112})$	$w_3(\frac{1}{5}a_{111}+\frac{3}{5}a_{112}$ $+\frac{1}{2}a_{122})$	$w_4(\frac{1}{20}a_{111}+\frac{9}{20}a_{112}$ $+\frac{9}{20}a_{122}+\frac{1}{20}a_{222})$
a_{112}		$w_3(\frac{1}{5}a_{111}+\frac{3}{5}a_{112}$ $+\frac{1}{5}a_{122})$	$w_4(\frac{1}{20}a_{111}+\frac{9}{20}a_{112}$ $+\frac{9}{20}a_{122}+\frac{1}{20}a_{222})$	$w_3(\frac{1}{5}a_{112}+\frac{3}{5}a_{122}$ $+\frac{1}{5}a_{222})$
a_{122}			$w_3(\frac{1}{5}a_{111}+\frac{3}{5}a_{112}$ $+\frac{1}{5}a_{122})$	$\frac{w_2}{2}(a_{122}+a_{222})$
a_{222}				$w_1 a_{222}$

Table-4

In this case transformation (3) does not help in the reduction of equation (2).

Hence we seek a general transformation of the basis in the form

$$\begin{aligned} c_0 &= a_{111} \\ c_1 &= ka_{111} - a_{112} \\ c_2 &= k_1 a_{111} + k_2 a_{112} + a_{112} \\ c_3 &= r_1 a_{111} + r_2 a_{112} + r_3 a_{122} - a_{222} \end{aligned} \qquad ...(5)$$

$$c_0 c_1 = a_{111}\,(ka_{111} - a_{112})$$

$$= \frac{w_2}{2}[(\frac{2kw_1}{w_2} - 1)a_{111} - a_{112}]$$

Choose k such that

$$k = \frac{w_2}{2k_1 - k_2} \qquad ...(6)$$

\

$$c_1 = \frac{w_2}{2w_1 - w_2}a_{111} - a_{112}$$

$$c_2 = k_1 a_{111} + k_2 a_{112} + a_{122}$$

$$= (k_1 w_1 + \frac{k_2 w_2}{2} + \frac{w_3}{5}) a_{111} + \left(\frac{k_2 w_2}{2} + \frac{3}{5}\right) w_3 a_{112} + \frac{w_3}{5} a_{112}$$

Choose k_1, k_2 such that

$$k_1 w_1 + \frac{k_2 w_2}{2} + \frac{w_3}{5} = k_1 \frac{w_3}{5} \qquad \text{...(7)}$$

$$\frac{k_2 w_2}{2} + \frac{3}{5} w_3 = k_2 \frac{w_3}{5}$$

$$k_2 = \frac{6}{2w_3 - 5w_3} w_3 \qquad \text{...(8)}$$

Putting the value of k_2 in (7)

$$k_1 w_1 + \frac{3w_3 w_2}{(2w_3 - 5w_2)} + \frac{w_3}{5} = k_1 \frac{w_3}{5}$$

$$k_1 = \frac{2w_2(w_3 + 5w_2)}{(2w_3 - 5w_2)(w_3 - 5w_1)}$$

Hence

$$c_2 = \frac{2w_3(w_3 + 5w_2)}{(2w_3 - 5w_2)(w_3 - 5w_1)} a_{111} + \frac{6w_3}{(2w_3 - 5w_2)} a_{112} + a_{122}$$

and $c_0 c_2 = \frac{w_3}{5} c_2$

$$c_0 c_3 = a_{111} \, (r_1 a_{111} + r_2 a_{112} + r_3 a_{122} - a_{222})$$

$$= r_1 w_1 a_{111} + r_2 \frac{w_2}{2}(a_{111} + a_{112}) + r_3 w_3 (\frac{1}{5} a_{111} + \frac{3}{5} a_{112} + 1/5 a_{122})$$

$$- \; w_4 (\frac{1}{20} a_{111} + \frac{9}{20} a_{112} + \frac{9}{20} a_{122} + \frac{1}{20} a_{222})$$

$$= (r_1 w_1 + \frac{r_2 w_2}{2} + \frac{r_3 w_3}{5} - \frac{w_4}{20}) a_{111} + (\frac{r_2 w_2}{2} + \frac{3}{5} r_3 w_3$$

$$-\frac{9w_4}{20})a_{112}+(\frac{r_3w_3}{5},\frac{9w_4}{20})a_{122}-\frac{w_4}{20}a_{222}$$

Choose r_1, r_2, r_3 such that

$$\frac{r_3w_3}{5}-\frac{9w_4}{20} = \frac{r_3w_4}{20} \quad ...(10)$$

$$\frac{r_2w_2}{2}+\frac{3}{5}r_3w_3-\frac{9w_4}{20} = \frac{r_2w_4}{20} \quad ...(11)$$

$$r_1w_1+\frac{r_2w_2}{2}+\frac{r_3w_3}{5}-\frac{w_4}{20} = \frac{r_1w_4}{20} \quad ...(12)$$

From (10)

$$r_3(\frac{w_4}{20}-\frac{w_3}{5}) = \frac{-9w_4}{20}$$

$$r_3\,(w_4-4w_3) = 9w_4$$

$$r_3 = \frac{-9w_4}{w_4-4w_3} \quad ...(13)$$

From (11)

$$r_2(\frac{w_4}{20}-\frac{w_2}{2}) = \frac{-3}{5}.\frac{9w_4w_3}{w_4-4w_3}-\frac{9w_4}{20}$$

$$r_2 = \frac{-9w_4(8w_3+w_4)}{(w_4-4w_3)(w_4-10w_2)} \quad ...(14)$$

From (12)

$$r_1(\frac{w_4}{20}-w_1) = -\frac{2}{2}.\frac{w_4w_2(8w_3+w_4)}{(w_4-4w_3)(w_4-10w_2)}-\frac{9}{5}\frac{w_4w_3}{w_4-4w_3}-\frac{w_4}{20}$$

$$= -w_4.\frac{9w_2(8w_3+w_4)+36w_3(w_4-10w_2)+(w_4-4w_3)(w_4-10w_2)}{20(w_4-4w_3)(w_4-10w_2)}$$

Denominator

$$= 90w_2(8w_3+w_4)+(w_4-10w_2)\,(w_4+32w_3)$$

$$= w_4^2 + 32w_4w_3 + 80w_3w_4 + 400w_2w_{3.}$$

$$r_1 = \frac{-w_4(w_4^2 + 32w_4w_3 + 80w_2w_4 + 400w_2w_3)}{(w_4 - 20w_1)(w_4 - 10w_2)(w_4 - 4w_3)} \quad ...(15)$$

Putting the values $k, k_1, k_2, r_1, r_2, r_3$ from (6), (9), (8), (15), (14) and (13)and we get the transformation

$$c = a_{111}$$

$$c_1 = \frac{w_2}{2w_1 - w_2} a_{111} - a_{112}$$

$$c_2 = \frac{2w_3(w_3 + 5w_2)}{(2w_3 - 5w_2)(w_3 - 5w_1)} a_{111} + \frac{6w_3}{(2w_3 - 5w_2)} a_{112} + a_{122}$$

$$c_3 = \frac{-w_4(w_4^2 + 32w_4w_3 + 80w_2w_4 + 400w_2w_3)}{(w_4 - 20w_1)(w_4 - 10w_2)(w_4 - 4w_3)} a_{111}$$

$$- \frac{9w_4(8w_3 + w_4)}{(w_4 - 4w_3)(w_4 - 10w_2)} a_{112} - \frac{9w_4}{(w_4 - 4w_3)} a_{122} - a_{222}$$

also we have,

$$a_{111} = c_0$$

$$c_{112} = \frac{w_2}{2w_1 - w_2} c_0 - c_1$$

$$a_{122} = \frac{-2w_3(w_3 + 5w_2)}{(2w_3 - 5w_2)(w_3 - 5w_1)} a_{111} - \frac{6w_3}{2w_3 - 5w_2} a_{112} + c_2$$

$$= -\left[\frac{2w_3(w_3 + 5w_2)}{(2w_3 - 5w_2)(w_3 - 5w_1)} + \frac{6w_2w_3}{(2w_3 - 5w_2)(2w_1 - w_2)}\right] c_0$$

$$+ \frac{6w_3}{2w_3 - 5w_2} c_1 + c_2$$

$$a_{122} = \frac{2w_3(w_1 + w_2)}{(w_3 - 5w_1)(w_2 - 2w_1)} c_0 + \frac{6w_3}{(2w_3 - 5w_2)} c_1 + c_2$$

$$a_{222}=\frac{-w_4(w_4^2+32w_1w_3+80w_2w_4+400w_2w_3)}{(w_4-20w_1)(w_4-10w_2)(w_4-4w_3)}a_{111}$$

$$=\frac{9w_4(8w_3+w_4)}{(w_4-4w_3)(w_4-10w_2)}a_{112}-\frac{9w_4}{(w_4-9w_3)}a_{112}-c_3$$

Substituting for a_{111}, a_{112}, a_{122} in the above expression, we have

$$a_{222}=\frac{-w_4(w_4^2+32w_4w_3+80w_2w_4+400w_2w_3)}{(w_4-20w_1)(w_4-10w_2)(w_4-4w_3)}c_0$$

$$-\frac{9w_4(8w_3+w_4)}{(w_4-4w_3)(w_4-10w_2)}\left(\frac{w_2}{2w_1-w_2}c_0-c_1\right)=\frac{w_4}{w_4-4w_3}$$

$$=\frac{-(w_4^2+32w_4w_3+80w_2w_4+400w_2w_3}{(w_4-20w_1)w_4-10w_3}-\frac{9(8w_3+w_4)w_2}{(w_4-10w_2)(2w_1-w_2)}$$

$$-\frac{9(2w_3)w_1+w_2)}{(w_3-5w_1)(w_2-2w_1)}]$$

$$c_0+\frac{9w_4}{w_4-4w_3}\left(\frac{8w_3+w_4}{w_4-10w_2}-\frac{6w_3}{2w_3-5w_2}\right)c_1$$

$$-\frac{9w_4}{w_4-4w_3}c_2-c_3$$

Hence the inverse of the transformation(16) is

$$a_{111}=c_0$$

$$a_{112}=\frac{w_2}{2w_1-w_2}c_0-c_1$$

$$a_{122}=\frac{2w_3(w_1+w_2)}{(w_3-5w_1)(w_2-2w_1)}c_0+\frac{6w_3}{(2w_3-5w_2)}c_1+c_2$$

$$a_{222}=\frac{w_4}{(w_4-4w_3)(w_4-20w_1)(w_4-10w_2)(w_2-2w_1)(w_3-5w_1)}$$

$$[(w_4^2+32w_4w_3+80w_2w_4+400w_2w_3)$$

$$(w_2-2w_1)(w_2-5w_1)+9(8w_2w_3+w_4w_2)$$

$$(w_4-20w_1)(w_3-5w_1)+9(2w_1w_3+2w_2w_3)(w_4-20w_1)$$

$$(w_4-10w_2)]c_0+\frac{9w_4(4w_3+5w_2)}{(w_4-10w_2)(5w_2-2w_3)}c_1-\frac{9w_4}{w_4-4w_3}c_2-c_3$$

How the new multiplication table is

	c_0	c_1	c_2	c_3
c_0	w_1c_0	$\frac{1}{2}w_2c_1$	$\frac{1}{5}w_3c_2$	$\frac{1}{20}w_4c_3$
c_1		$1_0c_0+1_1c_1+1_2c_2+1_3c_3$	$m_0c_0+m_1c_1+m_2c_2+m_3c_3$	$n_0c_0+n_1c_1+n_2c_2+n_3c_3$
c_2			$p_0c_0+p_1c_1+p_2c_2p_3c_3$	$q_0c_0+q_1c_1+a_2c_2+q_3c_3$
c_3				$r_0c_0+r_1c_1+r_2c_2+r_3c3$

Table-5

Remarks : 1. In the above table 1'^s^, m'^s, n'^s, p'^s, q'^s and r'^s are rational function of w_1, w_2, w_3, w_4.

2. The transformation (16) and(17) are free from the singularities only if

$$2w_1\neq w_2, 2w_3\neq 5w_2, w_3\neq 5w_1$$

$$w_4\neq 20w_1, 10w_2, 4w_3, 9w_3$$

3. If $w_1=w_2=w_3=w_4$, then (16) reduced to (3).

Reduction of the equation (1)

Let $x_1a_{111}+x_2a_{112}+x_3a_{122}+a_{222}$ be the initial sate of the population.

$$\text{Then } x= x_1c_0+x_2\left(\frac{w_2}{2w_1-w_2}c_0-c_1\right)+x_3\left[\frac{2w_3(w_1+w_2)}{(w_3-5w_1)(w_2-2w_1)}c_0\right.$$

$$\left.+\frac{6w_3}{(2w_3-5w_2)}c_1+c_2\right]$$

$$\frac{w_4}{(w_4-4w_3)(w_4-20w_1)(w_4-10w_2)(w_2-2w_1)(w_3-5w_1)}$$

$$[(w_4^2 32w_4w_3 + 80w_2w_4 + 400w_2w_3)(w_2 - 2w_1)(w_3 - 5w_1)$$

$$+9(8w_2w_3 + w_4w_2)(w_4 - 20w_1)(w_3 - 5w_1) + 9$$

$$(2w_1w_3 + 2w_2w_3)(w_4 - 20w_1)$$

$$(w_4 - 10w_2]c_0 + \frac{9w_4(4w_3 + 5w_2)}{(w_4 - 10w_2)(5w_2 - 2w_3)}c_1 - \frac{9w_4}{w_4 - 4w_3}c_2 - c_3$$

$= y_0c_0 + y_1c_1 + y_2c_2 + c_3$, from the equation (16)

where

$$y_0 = x_1 + \frac{w_2}{2w_1 - w_2}x_2 + \frac{2w_3(w_1 + w_2)}{(w_3 - 5w_1)(w_2 - 2w_1)}x_3$$

$$+ w_4[(w_4 - 4w_3)(w_4 - 20w_1)(w_4 - 10w_2)(w_2 - 2w_1)(w_3 - 5w_1)]^{-1}$$

$$[w_4^2 + 32w_3w_4 + 80w_2w_4 + 400w_2w_3)(w_2 - 2w_1)(w_3 - 5w_1)$$

$$+9(8w_2\,w_3 + w_2w_4)(w_4 - 20w_1)(w_3 - 5w_1) + 9(2w_1w_3 + 2w_2w_3)$$

$$(w_4 - 20w_1)(w_4 - 10w_2)]$$

$$y_1 = -x_2 + \frac{6w_3}{2w_3 - 5w_2}x_3 + \frac{9w_4(4w_3 + 5w_2)}{(w_4 - 10w_2)(5w_2 - 2w_3)}$$

$$y_2 = x_3 - \frac{9w_4}{w_4 - 4w_3}$$

\ $x^2 = \frac{1}{k}(y_0c_0 + y_1c_1 + y_2c_2 + c_3)^2$, where k is the coefficient of c_3 in the expansion of

$$(y_0c_0 + y_1c_1 + y_2c_2 + c_3)^2$$

i.e. $$x^2 = \frac{1}{k}(y_0^2\,c_0^2 + y_1^2c_1^2 + y_2^2c_2^2 + c_3^2 + 2y_0y_1c_0c_1 + 2y_0y_2c_0c_2$$

$$+2y_1y_2c_1c_2 + 2y_0c_0c_3 + 2y_1c_1c_3 + 2y_2c_2c_3)$$

$$= \frac{1}{k}[(y_0^2 w_1 c_0 + y_1^2(1_0 c_0 + 1_1 c_1 + 1_3 c_3) + y_2^2(p_0 c_0 + p_1 c_1 + p_2 c_2$$

$$+ p_3 c_3) + r_0 c_0 + r_1 c_1 + r_2 c_2 + r_3 c_3 + 2y_0 y_1 w_2 c_1$$

$$+ \frac{2}{5} y_0 y_2 w_3 c_2 + 2y_1 y_2 (n_0 c_0 + n_1 c_1 + n_2 c_2 + n_3 c_3)$$

$$+ \frac{1}{10} y_0 w_4 c_3 + 2y_1 (n_0 c_0 + n_1 c_1 + n_2 c_2 + n_3 c_3)$$

$$+ 2y_2 (q_0 c_0 + a_1 c_1 + q_2 c_2 + q_3 c_3)]$$

$$= \frac{1}{k}[(y_0^2 w_1 + y_1^2 1_0 + y_2^2 p_0 + r_0 + 2y_1 y_2 n_0 + 2y_1 n_0 + 2y_2 q_0) c_0$$

$$+ (y_1^2 1_1 + y_2^2 p_1 + r_1 + y_0 y_1 w_2 + 2y_1 y_2 n_1 + 2y_1 n_1 + 2y_2 q_1) c_1$$

$$+ (y_1^2 1_2 + y_2^2 p_2 + r_2 + \frac{2}{5} y_0 y_2 w_3 + 2y_1 y_2 n_2 + 2y_1 n_2 + 2y_2 q_2) c_2$$

$$+ (y_1^2 1_3 + y_2^2 p_3 + r_3 + 2y_1 y_2 n_3 + \frac{1}{10} y_0 w_4 + 2y_1 n_3 + 2y_2 q_3) c_3]$$

$$= \frac{y_0^2 w_1 + y_1^2 1_0 + y_2^2 p_0 + r_0 + 2y_1 y_2 n_0 + 2y_1 n_0 + 2y_0 q_0}{\frac{1}{10} y_0 w_4 + 2y_1 n_3 + 2y_2 q_3 + y_1^2 1_3 + y_2^2 p_3 + r_3 + 2y_1 y_2 n_3} c_0$$

$$+ \frac{y_1^2 1_1 + y_2^2 p_1 + r_1 + y_0 y_1 w_2 + 2y_1 y_2 n_1 + 2y_1 n_1 + 2y_2 q_1}{\frac{1}{10} y_0 w_4 + 2y_1 n_3 + 2y_2 q_3 + y_1^2 1_3 + y_2^2 p_3 + r_3 + 2y_1 y_2 n_3} c_1$$

$$+ \frac{y_1^2 1_2 + y_2^2 p_2 + r_2 + \frac{2}{5} y_0 y_2 w_3 + 2y_1 y_2 n_2 + 2y_1 n_2 + 2y_2 q_2}{\frac{1}{10} y_0 w_4 + 2y_1 n_3 + 2y_2 q_3 + y_1^2 1_3 + y_2^2 p_3 + r_3 + 2y_1 y_2 n_3}$$

Remark : The above equation is not in the normalized form.

5.4. Equalibria of the Hexaploid Population

Equilibrium states of hexaploid populations correspond to th idempotents in the algebra which describe the inheritance of the population. Clearly the idempotents are the fixed points of the evolution transformation defined by the evolution equation.

In this chapter we find equilibrim of the hexaploid population by obtaining fixed point of the evolution transformation using Brouwer's fixed point, theorem.

The equilibria will be obtained under the assumption, that two zygotes having same alleles have identical segregation behaviour and the segregation behaviour of a zygote remains unchanged if the alleles are interchanged.Idempotents in the algebra are given by

$$(x_1a_{111}+x_2a_{112}+x_3a_{122}+x_4a_{222})^2(x_1a_{111}+x_2a_{112}+x_3a_{122}+x_4a_{222})$$

i.e. $x_1^2a_{111}w_1+x_2^2w_3(\frac{1}{5}a_{111}+\frac{3}{5}a_{112}+\frac{1}{5}a_{122})+x_3^2w_3(\frac{1}{5}a_{112}+\frac{3}{5}a_{122}$

$$+\frac{1}{5}a_{222})+x_4^2w_1a_{222}+x_1x_2w_2(a_{111}+a_{112})+2x_1x_3w_3(\frac{1}{5}a_{111}$$

$$+\frac{3}{5}a_{112}+\frac{1}{5}a_{122})+2x_2x_4w_3(\frac{1}{5}a_{112}+\frac{3}{5}a_{122}+\frac{1}{5}a_{222})$$

$$+\ 2x_1x_4w_4(\frac{1}{20}a_{111}+\frac{9}{20}a_{112}+\frac{9}{20}a_{122}+\frac{1}{20}a_{222})$$

$$+\ 2x_2x_3w_4(\frac{1}{20}a_{111}+\frac{9}{20}a_{112}+\frac{9}{20}a_{122}+\frac{1}{20}a_{222})+w_2x_3x_4(a_{122}+a_{222})$$

$$=(x_1a_{111}+x_2a_{112}+x_3a_{122}+x_4a_{222})$$

i.e. $(x_1^2w_1+\frac{1}{5}x_2^2w_3+x_1x_2w_2+\frac{2}{5}x_1x_3w_3+\frac{1}{10}x_2x_4w_4+\frac{1}{10}x_2x_3w_4)^{a_{111}}$

$$+(\frac{3}{5}x_2^2w_3+\frac{1}{5}x_3^2w_3+x_1x_2w_2+\frac{6}{5}x_1x_3w_3+\frac{2}{5}x_2x_4w_3+\frac{9}{10}x_1x_4w_4$$

$$+\ \frac{9}{10}x_3x_3w_4)a_{112}+(\frac{1}{5}x_2^2w_3+\frac{3}{5}x_2^2\,w_3+\frac{2}{5}x_1x_3w_3+\frac{6}{5}x_2x_4w_3$$

$$+\frac{9}{10}x_1x_4w_4+\frac{9}{10}x_2x_3w_4+x_3x_4w_2)a_{122}+(\frac{1}{5}x_3^2w_3+x_4^2w_1$$

$$+\frac{2}{5}x_2x_4w_3+\frac{1}{10}x_1x_4w_4+\frac{1}{10}x_2x_3w_4+x_3x_4w_2)a_{222}$$

$$=(x_1a_{111}+x_2a_{112}+x_3a_{122}+x_4a_{222})$$

$$x_1^2w_1+\frac{1}{5}x_2^2w_3+x_1x_2w_2+\frac{2}{5}x_1x_3w_3+\frac{1}{10}x_1x_4w_4+\frac{1}{10}x_2x_3w_4=x_1 \quad ..(1)$$

$$\frac{3}{5}x_2^2w_3+\frac{1}{5}x_3^2w_3+x_1x_2w_2+\frac{6}{5}x_1x_3w_3+\frac{2}{5}x_2x_4w_3+\frac{9}{10}x_1x_4w_4$$

$$+\frac{9}{10}x_2x_3w_4=x_2 \quad ....(2)$$

$$\frac{1}{5}x_2^2w_3+\frac{3}{5}x_3^2w_3+\frac{2}{5}x_2x_4w_3+\frac{9}{10}x_1x_4w_4+\frac{9}{10}x_2x_3w_4+x_3x_4w_2=x_3$$

...(3)

$$\frac{1}{5}x_3^2w_3+x_4^2w_1+\frac{2}{5}x_2x_4w_3+\frac{1}{10}x_1x_4w_4+\frac{1}{10}x_2x_3w_4+x_3x_4w_2=x_4 \quad ...(4)$$

Substracting equation (4) from (1) and we get

$$10w_1(x_1^2-x_4^2)+2w_3(x_2^2-x_3^2)+4w_3(x_1x_3-x_2x_4)$$

$$+10w_2(x_1x_2-x_3x_4)=10(x_1-x_4) \quad ...(5)$$

Again substracting (3) from (2) we get

$$4w_3(x_2^2-x_3^2)+10w_2(x_1x_2-x_3x_4)+8w_3(x_1x_3-x_2x_4)=10\,(x_2-x_3) ...(6)$$

We assume that

$x_1=x_4$ then from (5) and (6),we have

$(x_2-x_3)\,[2w_3\,(x_2+x_3)-4xw_3+10xw_2]=0$ ...(5[1])

$(x_2-x_3)\,[\,4w_3\,(x_2+x_3)+10w_2x-8xw_3-10]=0$ ...(6[1])

Thus, $x_2-x_3=0$ or $2w_3\,(x_2+x_3)-4xw_3+10xw_2=0$ ...(7)

and $2w_3\,(x_2+x_3)-4xw_3+5xw_2-5=0$ ...(8)

Substract equation (8) from (7)

$$10xw_2 - 5xw_2 + 5 = 0$$

$$x = -\frac{1}{w_2} \qquad \text{...(9)}$$

Putting the value of x in equation (7), we get

$$x_2 + x_3 = \frac{-2}{w_2} + \frac{5}{w_3} \qquad \text{...(10)}$$

If $x_2 = x_3 = y$, then from (5) and (6),we have

$$x_1 - x_4 = 0 \text{ or } 5w_1(x_1 + x_4) + 2yw_3 + 5yw_2 - 5 = 0$$

Since $y \square 0$, $5w_2 + 4w_3 \square 0$

We can not have(9) and (10)

Hence we have only two cases

Case-I : $x_1 = x_4$; $x_2 = x_3$

First we prove the following.

Theorem-I : In the algebra of hexaploids given by table – 2, there is an indempotent of the form

$$x_1 a_{111} + x_2 a_{112} + x_2 a_{122} + x_1 a_{222}$$

$$2x_1 + 2x_2 = 1; \text{if } w_1, w_2, w_3, w_4 > 0$$

Proof : The normalized equation transformation

$f : x \square \dfrac{x^2}{\| x^2 \|}$ is given by

$$\frac{x^2}{\| x^2 \|} = \frac{1}{w}[(x_1^2 w_1 + \frac{1}{5}x_2^2 w_3 + x_1 x_2 w_2 + \frac{2}{5}x_1 x_2 w_3 + \frac{1}{10}x_1^2 w_4$$

$$+ \frac{1}{10}x_2^2 w_4) a_{111} + (\frac{3}{5}x_2^2 w_3 + \frac{1}{5}x_2^2 w_3 + x_1 x_2 w_2$$

$$+ \frac{6}{5}x_1 x_2 w_3 + \frac{2}{5}x_1 x_2 w_3 + \frac{9}{10}x_1^2 w_4 + \frac{9}{10}x_2^2 w_4) a_{112}$$

$$+ (\frac{1}{5}x_2^2 w_3 + \frac{3}{5}x_2^2 w_3 + \frac{2}{5}x_1 x_2 w_3 + \frac{6}{5}x_1 x_2 w_3 + \frac{9}{10}x_1^2 w_4$$

$$+\frac{9}{10}x_2^2w_4+2x_1x_2w_2)a_{122}+(\frac{1}{5}x_2^2w_3+x_1^2w_1$$

$$+\frac{2}{5}x_1x_2w_3+\frac{1}{10}x_1^2w_4+\frac{1}{10}x_2^2w_4+x_1x_2w_2)a_{222}]$$

Where $w=2x_1^2w_1+2x_1^2w_4+2x_2^2w_3+2x_2^2w_4+4x_1x_2w_3+5x_1x_2w_2$

Clearly the coordinate function

$$f_1(x_1,x_2,x_2,x_1)=\frac{1}{w}[(x_1^2w_1+\frac{1}{5}x_2^2w_3+x_1x_2x_2+\frac{2}{5}x_1x_2w_3$$

$$\frac{1}{10}x_1^2w_4+\frac{1}{10}x_2^2w_4)]$$

$$f_2(x_1,x_2,x_2,x_1)=\frac{1}{w}[(\frac{3}{5}x_2^2w_3+\frac{1}{5}x_2^2w_3+x_1x_2w_2+\frac{6}{5}x_1x_2w_3$$

$$+\frac{2}{5}x_1x_2w_3+\frac{9}{10}x_1^2w_4+\frac{9}{10}x_2^2w_4)]$$

$$f_3(x_1,x_2,x_2,x_1)=f_2(x_1,x_2,x_2,x_1)$$

$$f_4(x_1,x_2,x_2,x_1)=f_1(x_1,x_2=\frac{1}{2},x_3x_1)$$

are continuous under the conditions of the theorem, Hence the function f is continuous

Domain of the function f

$$D=\{(x_1,x_2,x_2,x_1)\notin IR^4:x_1+x_2=\frac{1}{2},x_1,x_2\notin IR\}$$

is obtained linear constraint on R^4 and is it so convex.

Since 0 £ × £ 1, D is bounded.

To prove that D is closed, it is sufficient to show that D^c is open.

Let $(x_1,x_2,x_2,x_1)\varepsilon D^c$

The $x_1+x_2\neq\frac{1}{2}$

If $(x_1^1, x_2^1, x_2^1, x_1^1)\varepsilon D$, then $x_1^1 + x_2^1 = \frac{1}{2}$

Consider an open sphere S with centre (x_1, x_2, x_2, x_1) and radius

$\frac{1}{2} - (x_1 + x_2)$

If S contains a point then

$(x_1^1, x_2^1, x_2^1, x_1^1)\varepsilon D$ then

$$[(x_1, x_2, x_2, x_1), (x_1^1, x_2^1, x_2^1, x_1^1) <] \frac{1}{2} - (x_1 + x_2)$$

$$2(x_1 - x_1^1)^2 + 2(x_2 - x\frac{1}{2})^2 < [\frac{1}{2} - (x_1 + x_2)]^2$$

$$[(x_1 + x_2) - (x_1^1 + x\frac{1}{2})]^2 + (x_1 - x_1^1 - x_2 + x_2^1)^2 < [\frac{1}{2} - (x_1 + x_2)^2]$$

$$[\frac{1}{2} - (x_1 + x_2)]^2 + (x_1 - x_1^1 - x_2 + x_2^1)^2 < [(\frac{1}{2} - (x_1 + x_2)]^2$$

which is a contradiction.

Thus there exist a who S of each point of D^c which is entirely contained in D^c. i.e. D^c is open and so D is a closed set.

Hence by Broswerts fixed point theorem it follows that *f* as a fixed point which is an indempotent in the algebra.

Hence the theorem.

How we proceed to obtain the indempotent.We have

$$(w_1 + \frac{1}{10}w_4)x_1^2 + (w_2 + \frac{2}{5}w_3)x_1x_2 + (\frac{1}{5}w_3 + \frac{1}{10}w_4)x_2^2 - x_1 \qquad ...(1^1)$$

$$\frac{9}{10}w_4x_1^2 + (\frac{8}{5}w_3 + w_2)x_1x_2 + (\frac{4}{5}w_3 + \frac{9}{10}w_4)x_2^2 = x_2 \qquad ...(2^1)$$

Now (1) $x\frac{9}{10}w_4 - (2')x(w_1 + \frac{1}{10}w_4)$ yields

$$\frac{9}{10}w_4(w_2+\frac{2}{5}w_3)x_1x_2+\frac{9}{10}w_4(\frac{1}{5}w_3+\frac{1}{10}w_4)x_2^2$$

$$-(w_1+\frac{1}{10}w_4)(\frac{8}{5}w_3+w_2)x_1x_2-(w_1+\frac{1}{10}w_4)(\frac{4}{5}w_3+\frac{9}{10}w_4)x_2^2$$

$$=\frac{9}{10}w_4x_1-(w_1+\frac{1}{10}w_4)x_2 \qquad ...(3)$$

i.e. $$x_1[\frac{9}{10}w_4(w_2+\frac{2}{5}w_3)x_2-(w_1+\frac{1}{10}w_4)(\frac{3}{5}w_3+w_2)x_2-\frac{9}{10}w_4]$$

$$=(w_1+\frac{1}{10}w_4)(\frac{4}{5}w_3+\frac{9}{10}w_4)x_2^2-\frac{9}{10}w_4(\frac{1}{5}w_3+\frac{9}{10}w_4)x_2^2$$

$$-(w_1+\frac{1}{10}w_4)x_2$$

Put $$\text{K}=\frac{9}{10}w_4(w_2+\frac{2}{5}w_3)$$

$$\text{M}=(w_1+\frac{1}{10}w_4)(\frac{8}{5}w_3+w_2)$$

$$\text{N}=(w_1+\frac{1}{10}w_4)(\frac{4}{5}w_3+\frac{1}{10}w_4) \qquad ...(4)$$

$$\text{P}=\frac{9}{10}w_4(\frac{1}{5}w_3+\frac{1}{10}w_4)$$

and $$\text{R}=(w_1+\frac{1}{10}w_4)$$

How, $x_1(kx_2-\text{M}x_2-\frac{9}{10}w_4]=\text{N}x_2^2-px_2^2-\text{R}x_2$

$$x_1=\frac{\text{N}x_2^2-px_2^2-\text{R}x_2}{\text{K}x_2-\text{M}x_2-\frac{9}{10}w_4} \qquad ...(5)$$

Putting the value of x_1 in equation (2′) and we get

$$\frac{9}{10}w_4x_1^2+(\frac{8}{5}w_3+w_2)x_1x_2+(\frac{4}{5}w_3+\frac{9}{10}w_4)x_2^2=x_2$$

$$\frac{9}{10}w_4[\frac{Mx_2^2+Px_2^2-Rx_2}{Kx_2-Mx_2-\frac{9}{10}w_4}]^2+(\frac{8}{5}w_3+w_2)[\frac{Mx_2^2-Px_2^2-Rx_2}{Kx_2-Mx_2-\frac{9}{10}w_4}]x_2$$

$$+(\frac{4}{5}w_3+\frac{9}{10}w_4)x_2^2=x_2$$

$$\frac{9}{10}w_4x_2(Mx_2-Px_2-R)^2+(\frac{2}{5}w_3+w_2)(Mx_2-Px_2-R)$$

$$(Kx_2-Mx_2-\frac{9}{10}w_4)x_2+(\frac{4}{5}w_3+\frac{9}{10}w_4)(Mx_2-Px_2-R)^2x_2$$

$$=(Kx_2-Mx_2-\frac{9}{10}w_4)^2$$

i.e. $$\frac{9}{10}w_4(M^2x_2^2+P^2x_2^2+R^2-2Mx_2^2+2PRx_2-2MRx_2)x_2$$

$$+x_2(\frac{8}{5}w_3\,Mx_2-\frac{8}{5}W_3Px_2-\frac{8}{5}w_3R+w_2\,Mx_2-w_2Px_2-w_2R)$$

$$Kx_2-Mx_2-\frac{9}{10}w_4)+(\frac{4}{5}w_3x_2+\frac{9}{10}w_4x_2)(M^2x_2^2+P^2x_2^2+R_2^2MPx_2^2$$

$$+2PRx_2-2MRx_2)=(Kx_2-Mx_2-\frac{9}{10}w_4)^2$$

i.e. $$(\frac{9}{10}W_4M^2+\frac{9}{10}W_4P^2-\frac{9}{5}W_4\,MP+\frac{8}{5}W_3\,MK-\frac{8}{5}W_3M^2-\frac{8}{5}W_3PK$$

$$+\frac{8}{5}PM+W_2\,MK-W_2M^2-W_2KP+W_2MP+\frac{4}{5}W_3M^2+\frac{4}{5}W_3P^2$$

$$-\frac{8}{5}W_3\,MP+\frac{9}{10}W_4M^2+\frac{9}{10}W_4P^2-\frac{8}{5}W_4MP)\,x_2^3+\{(\frac{9}{5}W_4PR$$

$$-\frac{8}{5}W_4MR-\frac{26}{25}w_3w_4\,M+\frac{36}{35}w_3w_4P-\frac{8}{5}w_3\,RK+\frac{8}{5}W_3RM-\frac{9}{10}w_4M$$

$$-\frac{9}{10}w_2w_4P-w_2KR+w_2RM+\frac{8}{5}w_3PR-\frac{8}{5}w_3MR+\frac{9}{10}w_4PR$$

$$-\frac{9}{10}w_4\,MR-(K-M)^2\}x_2^2+\{\frac{9}{10}w_4R^2+\frac{36}{25}w_3w_4+\frac{9}{10}w_2w_4R$$

$$+\frac{4}{5}w_3R^2+\frac{9}{10}w_4R^2+\frac{9}{5}(K-M)\}x_2-\frac{81}{100}w_4=0$$

5.5 Optimization of gamete frequencies in a hexaploid population

In section 4.5 of chapter we discused the optimization gamete frequencies in a tetrapliod population. The optimization of gamete frequencies under similar conditions can be discussed along the some lines.

Let x_1,x_2, x_3,x_4 be the frequncies of the gametes $a_1a_1a_1$, $a_1a_1a_2$, $a_1a_2a_2$ and $a_2a_2\,a_2$ in a population of hexaploids. Let the inheritance of the population be given by the table-2(Section 5.1).Them

(01) To obtain the values of x_1, x_2, x_3, x_4 in initial generation such that it gives maximum(or minimum) values of a particular gamete,say $a_1\,a_1\,a_1$ in the filial generation.

(02) To obtain the values of x_1, x_2, x_3, x_4 in initial generation 3 such that it gives maximum (or minimum values of a particular) gamete, say $a_1\,a_1\,a_1$ in the nth generation.

(03) To obtain the asympotic value of the frequency of $a_1\,a_1\,a_1$.

We can obtain the solution in the closed form of the problem (01), (02) and (03), following are the same logical steps as in the case of tetraploidy under the following conditions.

I. Zygotes (union of two gametes) containing same alleles have same segregation behaviour.

II. If the alleles are interchance then the segregation behaviour of zygote remains unchanged.

Condition (I) and (II)

□ $w_{11}=w_{44}=w_1$

$w_{12}=w_{21}=w_{34}=w_{43}=w_2$

$$w_{31} = w_{13} = w_{24} = w_{42} = w_{22}$$
$$= w_{33} = w_{3}$$
$$w_{14} = w_{41} = w_{13} = \mathrm{w}_{32} = w_{4}$$

III. $x_1 = x_4, x_2 = x_3$

In view of (I),(II) and (III), the normalised evolution equation is :

$$x_1^{(1)} a_{111} + x_2^{(1)} a_{112} + x_3^{(1)} a_{122} + x_4^{(1)} a_{222} = \frac{x^2}{\| x^2 \|}$$

$$= \frac{1}{w}[(x_1^2 w_1 + \frac{1}{5} x_2^2 w_3 + x_1 x_2 w_2 + \frac{2}{5} x_1 x_2 + \frac{1}{10} x_2^2 w_4) a_{111}$$

$$+ (\frac{3}{5} x_2^2 w_3 + \frac{1}{5} x_2^2 w_3 + x_1 x_2 w_2 + \frac{6}{5} x_1 x_2 w_3 + \frac{2}{5} x_1 x_2 w_3$$

$$+ \frac{9}{10} x_1^2 w_4 + \frac{9}{10} x_2^2 w_4) a_{112} + (\frac{1}{5} x_2^2 w_3 + \frac{3}{5} x_2^2 w_3 + \frac{2}{5} x_1 x_2 w_3$$

$$+ \frac{6}{5} x_1 x_2 w_3 + \frac{9}{10} x_1^2 w_4 + \frac{9}{10} x_2^2 w_4 + x_1 x_2 w_2) a_{122}$$

$$+ (\frac{1}{5} x_2^2 w_3 + x_1^2 w_1 \frac{2}{5} x_1 x_2 w_3 + \frac{1}{10} x_1^2 w_4 + \frac{1}{10} x_2^2 w_4 + x_1 x_2 w_3) a_{222}]$$

where

$$w = 2x_1^2 w_1 + 2x_1^2 w_4 + 2x_2^2 w_3 + 2x_2^2 w_d + 4x_1 x_2 w_3 + 4x_1 x_2 w_2 = a_1 a_1 a_1$$

$= a_{111}, a_1 a_1 a_2 = a_{112}$ etc. $x_1 + x_2 = \frac{1}{2}$. and

Since $x^{(1)}, x^{(2)} = \frac{1}{2}$, it is sufficient to considerthe maximum and minimum values of

$$x_1^{(1)} = f(x_1)$$

$$= \frac{1}{2}(x_1^2 w_1 + \frac{1}{5} x_2^2 w_3 + x_1 x_2 w_2 + \frac{2}{5} x_1 x_2 + \frac{1}{10} x_2^2 w_4)$$

Putting $x_2 = \frac{1}{2} - x_1$, we have

$$x_1^{(1)} = f(x_1) = \frac{A x_1^2 + Bx_1 + C}{A_1 x_1^2 + B_1 K_1 + C_1}$$

Where

$$A = w_1 - w_2 - \frac{1}{5} w_3 + \frac{1}{5} w_4$$

$$B = \frac{1}{2} w_2 - \frac{1}{10} w_4$$

$$C = \frac{1}{40}(2w_3 + w_4)$$

$$A_1 = 2(w_1 - 2w_2 - w_3 + 2w_4)$$

$$B_1 = 2(w_2 - w_4)$$

$$C_1 = \frac{1}{2}(w_3 + w_4) \qquad ...(1)$$

For simplicity we write x in place of x_1. Then we have to maximise or minimize

$$f(x) = \frac{Ax^2 + Bx + C}{A_1 x^2 B_1 x + C_1} \qquad ...(2)$$

where $0 \le x \le \frac{1}{2}$

since $0 \le x \le \frac{1}{2} \Rightarrow 0 \le f(x) \le \frac{1}{2}$

f is a continuous function defined on the closed and bounded (i.e. compact) interval $[0, \frac{1}{2}]$ in R, f attains its maximum and minimum values in $[0, \frac{1}{2}]$. We have

$$f^1(x) = \frac{(AB_1 - A_1B)x^2 - 2(CA_1 - C_1A) \times (BC_1 - B_1C)}{(A_1x^2 + B_1x + C_1)^2}$$

where

$$AB_1 - A_1B = w_1w_2 + \frac{3}{5}w_2w_3 + \frac{1}{5}w_3w_4 - \frac{9}{5}w_1w_4$$

$$BC_1 - B_1C = \frac{1}{20}(w_2w_3 + w_3w_4 + 3w_2w_4)$$

$$CA_1 - C_1A = \frac{1}{20}[6w_2w_3 + 3w_3w_4 - 9w_4w_1 - 8w_1w_3 + 8w_2w_4]$$

We propose to complete the solution in a subsequent work.

REFERENCES

1. Abraham, V.M. : Linearizing quadratic transformations in gematic algebras; Proc. London; Math. Sec. (3) 40 (ISBO) 346-63.

2. Abraham V.M. : The induced linear transformation in a gematic algebra, frec. London Math. Sec. (3) 40 (1960) 364-384.

3. Borisovich, YU.; Blisyakyov, M. ; Igrillvich, YA. Fomenko, T : Introduction to Tepology, NIR Publishers, Moscow, 1985.

4. Etherington, I.N.H. : Gemetic algebras, Prec. Roy, Sec.Edimburgh 69 (1939) 242-266.

5. Edwards, A.K.F. : Foundations of Mathematical genetics, Cambridge Ūniversity Press, 1977.

6. Portini, P. Berakat, R. R. : Gemetic algebras for tetraploidy with several Losi. J. Math. Biol. 9, 297-304 (1980)

7. Callais, B. : Selection with trumsation in autetetraploids comparison with diploids Theory. Appl. Gemet, 46 (1975), 387-394.

8. Gonshor, H. : Special train algebras arising in gemetic,Proc. Edinburgh Math. Sec. (2) 12 (1960) 41-53.

9. Gonshor,H. : Special train algebras arising in genetics II, Proc. Edinburgh Math. Sec. (2) 14 (1965), 333-338.

10. Gom shor, H. : Contributions to gemetic algebras,

Proc. Edinburgh Math. Sec. (2) 17 (1971) 289-298.

11. Holdane,J.B.S. : The conflict between inbreeding and Selection I, self fertilization; J. Genet. 54, 56-63.

12. Hayman, B.I. and Mather, K : The progress inbreeding when home zygotes are at a disadvantage; Heredity (1953), 7, 165-83.

13. Holgate, P. : Sequences of powers in genetic algebras; J. London Math. Sec. 42 (1967), 489-96.

14. Holgate, P. : Genetic algebras associated with Polyploidy. Proc. Edinburgh Math.Sec. (2) 15 (1966)1-9 corrigendum, Ibid. 17 (1970) 180.

15. Holgate, P. and Machado,S.D.A : Recombination between polyploid loci, J.Math. Biol. (1987) 25, 637-642.

16. Heuch, I. : The gemetic algebra for polyploidywith an arbitrary amount of double reduction, J.Math. Biol. 6 (1978) 343-352.

17. Heuch,I : An explicit formula for frequency changes in gemetic algebras, J. Math.Bio. 5(1977) 43-53.

18. Hill, R.R : Selection in autotetraploids. Theor. Appl. Genet. 41 (1971) 181-186.

19. Hill, R.R. and Haag, W.L. : Comparison of selection methods in autotetraplbids Crop. Science 14 (1974), 587-590.

20. Jha, K.K. : Advanced Topology, Nav Bharat Prakashan, Patna, Delhi 1984.

21. Kumar, Ram Awadhesh : On a non-linear difference equation in population genetics, The Mathematics Students, Vol. 58,(1991) Nos. 1-4 pp 134-138.

22. Parsons, P.A. : Equilibria in autotetraploids under natural selection for a simplified model of viabilities Biometrics 15 (1959), 20-29.

23. Pentony, S.J. and Semeta, E. : Partition of the genotypic variance and mean fitness change for autotetraploids,Biomeirische Zeitchrift 18 (1976), 301-311.

24. Ringwood, G.A. : Hypergemetric algebra and

mendelian gemetics,Archievfavour Wisknede (4), Vol.3, (1985) 69-83.

25. Swanometal, M.R. Simulated selection in autotetraploids populations, Crop. Science 14 (1974), 625-636.

26. Singh, M.K. : The gemetic algebra for polyploidy with several losi, J. Math Bio. (1987) 24, 723-727.

27. Singh, M.K. : Extending the theory of linearization ingematic algebra, Indian J.Pare and Appl. Math. (6) 530-538, June (1988).

28. Singh, M.K. and Kumar, Ram Awadesh : Equilibria of the tetraploid population with selection, Journal of Bihar Mathematical society,to appear.

29. Singh, S. and Prasad, R.L. : An aspect of the geometryof Hilbert spaces : Progress of Mathematics,Vol. 8, Vol 8, (11), (1974), 31-48.

30. Worz-Busekros, A. : Polypoidy with an arbitrary mixtureof chromosome and chromatid segregation, J. Math. Bio. 6 (1978), 353-365.

31. Wright, A.J. : Phenotypic selection in autopoly ploids, Heredity 35 (1975), 282-286.